SEARCH
for the
Signers

Enjoy the book!

Jennifer Epstein Rudnick

www.mascotbooks.com

Search for the Signers: Visiting the Graves of the Signers of the Declaration of Independence

For more information, please contact:
Mascot Books
620 Herndon Parkway, Suite 320
Herndon, VA 20170
info@mascotbooks.com

Library of Congress Control Number: 2020915778

CPSIA Code: PRV0521A
ISBN: 978-1-64307-570-9

Printed in the United States

To Rachel D'Ambrosio, for setting me on this path.

CONTENTS

I

How It All Got Started

I can pinpoint my interest in American history to the fifth grade. Other than the yearly telling of the Pilgrim story or explaining why we celebrate Washington's Birthday, it was my first exposure to studying American history and events, such as the American Revolution and the Civil War. I remember being shocked that each of these wars was more than just one big battle and that each lasted for years. My teacher that year, Ms. D., made all of these events come alive. Who would know then the impact she would have on my life?

That first year after my interest in history was sparked, I went on a weekend bus trip with my grandparents to Washington, DC. I was the only kid on the senior citizens bus tour and I remember all of the attention I received. We stayed at a hotel just across the river in Virginia with a revolving cocktail lounge on top. The view from that lounge was amazing, looking out over National Airport with planes landing and taking off. Just being in a cocktail lounge was memorable for a sixth-grader.

Everywhere I looked I could see the Washington Monument. It's ironic now, since I work in Washington, DC, and feel like I still can't escape from the Washington Monument.

My first trip to the capital city was fantastic. It was great to spend quality time with my grandparents and see the sights of Washington, DC. I have a picture of my stylish grandpa wearing a plaid jacket, while standing at John Kennedy's grave in Arlington Cemetery. Perhaps I was destined for such a project. I remember Grandpa had one of those cameras where you had to look down into it to take a picture. I never understood how those worked. We went all over the city, even down to Mount Vernon. The history bug had definitely bitten me and I took the camera with me everywhere. In fact, they teased me quite a bit in college and beyond because of my ever-present camera.

Fig 1: Grandpa Irving at Arlington Cemetery, 1982. All photos are taken by the author except where noted otherwise.

Through my years working seasonally for the National Park Service, I would come across others with similar interests. With common days off, we would hike around a battlefield or visit a historic site. We would spend our days off doing exactly what we did at work all day. We'd always have some minor adventure or new joke along the way that would be hard to forget. Like the day my friend Bert locked the keys in the car and we had to hang out in the New Hope Baptist Church waiting for the local sheriff to come help us, just two days before Christmas with an impending snowstorm. I am Jewish, so I learned all the specifics about Christian traditions from Bert as he explained what religious events were displayed in the church's stained-glass windows.

My friends probably sparked my interest in old cemeteries, as we looked for generals' graves or just wandered around through an old boneyard, as my friend Michael would call it. It was amazing to look at the dates on the stones, especially the really old ones, and imagine what happened to these people. I remember years ago, while in college, an old friend named Eric came to visit my home in Connecticut and told me how much he liked looking at old cemeteries. I took him to a few old graveyards in my area. I thought at the time it was rather strange and creepy that he was so interested in traipsing around these old cemeteries. Now look at me. I understand.

Fig 2: Eric and Jen at Gen. John Sedgwick's grave, Cornwall,
Connecticut, 1990

The Declaration of Independence has been a particular interest of
mine since I first saw the musical *1776* in a summer stock production.
I was in junior high and I loved the show so much that I told my social
studies teacher about it. The whole class then went to see the show. I had
to find the movie on VHS tape and once I accomplished that, my neigh-
bor made me a copy. I played the soundtrack until I knew all the songs by
heart. Any time I see *1776* playing anywhere nearby, I go to see the show.
Years ago, when it made a Broadway comeback, my mother and I made
the trip to New York to see it. My father and I saw a traveling version in
Hartford. There have been numerous local summer shows along the way.
I even saw the show at the historic Ford's Theatre in Washington, DC. I
have had movie-watching parties at my house in honor of the anniversary
of the Declaration signing. Nowadays it is difficult for people to watch
the movie with me since I know it so well and can recite the whole thing.

From this show I also developed a strong interest in the life of John Adams and what I feel are his under-appreciated contributions to our country's history. I felt this way long before it was popular to study John Adams. I wrote my high school senior year

Fig 3: Jen with author David McCullough, 2002 (photo by Ruth Epstein)

paper in 1989 on why Adams was underrated in American history. After his famous biography came out, I met author David McCullough at a history conference. While asking him to sign my copy of his Adams book I told him about that high school paper. McCullough said to me, "I guess you were ahead of your time." It was a proud moment to hear that from such a distinguished author.

Combining my love of traveling to historic sites, taking pictures, and studying about the Declaration of Independence is how this project was born. Officially, it started with a trip I took to Boston with my friends in October of 1999. Michael and Bert were fellow park rangers and traveling companions. We spent a week in the Boston area visiting historic sites. When I found three signers buried in one cemetery, I thought this might be an interesting idea; find and photograph all the graves of the signers of the Declaration of Independence. The funny thing is that when I returned home from that trip and started to think about it more seriously, I realized I had photos of four signers' graves already in my collection. So I was off.

Fig 4: Jen's father, Ed, 2002

A final necessary component for the successful completion of this project is a gene I attribute to my father—an obsessive trait. Once I get an idea there is no stopping me. While it may be a bizarre and slightly morbid concept to search out the graves of historically significant people, at least it is not a harmful habit. Luckily, I have found numerous friends willing to help me out and take part in this endeavor. They will be met along the way, as I promised each who helped me would be included in a book if ever I wrote one.

Who would have thought as I set out on this quest that I would be faced with so many different mysteries? I have found that what seemed like a fairly simple and straightforward task, with the exception of travel, has become much more complex. Fifty-six men signed the Declaration of Independence. They were all respected men in their colonies. Most were pretty well off financially, at least before the American Revolution. One would think such prominent men would have been honored in death.

Yet as I have searched out these signers' graves, I have found there is more to each story than a simple burial. Many of these men were removed from their original burial sites and moved to another location. Some are buried in cemeteries with such poor records that the exact burial place cannot be identified. Some graves may even be lost forever. My attempt to travel around the East Coast documenting the resting places of the founding fathers led to more questions than I could possibly have imagined. While I am sure many of these questions will remain unanswered, exploring the lives and deaths and beyond of these daring patriots has been a fascinating adventure.

II

The Dresser Drawer

P art of my father's legacy to me is the saver gene. Neither of us ever throws things away—we save everything. I have yet to figure out exactly why, before he married my mother, he used to save empty toothpaste tubes, but I do understand how hard it is to throw certain items out. Apparently it runs deeper genetically, as I learned when cleaning out my maternal grandparents' apartment. My grandfather had every credit card he had ever received and must have kept every piece of mail. So I must get this fine habit from both sides of the family.

In any case, since I had a computer desk without the typical desk drawers to hide junk in, I had a dresser that served as storage space. The second drawer, and eventually the fourth as well, was devoted to my developed rolls of film. I love to take pictures of my travels and my friends and family. I always used to tell my college roommates, when they were particularly annoyed by my hobby, that one day they would appreciate all of these photos. It is always neat to have pictures to look back on and remember fun occasions. In my mind the digital camera has been the greatest invention, saving me money and dresser drawer space.

When I first came up with the idea of collecting photographs of signers' graves, I thought back on previous travels. Without even consciously planning it, I had already taken some pictures of graves. I spent one evening rummaging through the dresser drawer to see exactly what was in there that might fit the collection.

If I were to pick the first photo I ever took of a Declaration signers' grave, I guess it would be Thomas Jefferson's. His grave is located at his home Monticello, outside of Charlottesville, Virginia, in a family plot. Being a highly visited tourist attraction, this was an easy grave to find and photograph. I have made many trips to Monticello. After my introduction to history in fifth grade I often was in charge of planning the family vacations. Usually it meant visiting some historic sites and occasionally included baseball games. Dad and I are big baseball fans.

Fig 5: Monticello, Charlottesville, Virginia

Often a trip to Independence Hall in Philadelphia, where the Declaration was debated and signed, was accompanied by an evening baseball game. My poor younger brother was dragged from historic site to ballpark. No wonder it is so hard to convince him to come visit me in Washington today. All of those family vacations did him in.

The family made a few trips to Monticello over the years. I compiled a photo album of pictures from all of the historic places I had visited, with many taken at Monticello. Jefferson's genius always strikes me there as I wander the beautiful grounds and tour the home with all its neat inventions. I feel there are certain places that all Americans should visit. I am sure my interest in history gives me a real bias, but I would have to put Monticello near the top of that list.

I felt so strongly about this that I insisted on taking my friend Amy to Monticello in the summer of 1992. Amy is from Washington state and was working with me for the summer at the Gettysburg Battlefield. I think it was one of her first trips to the East Coast. As the only one that summer with a car, I felt it was my duty to help Amy see as much of the historic East Coast as possible.

At the end of the summer, we planned this crazy whirlwind tour of Virginia. I think we started in Richmond and moved on to Williamsburg for dinner. Unknown to us at the time, we picked one of the fancier restaurants in Williamsburg to dine at, right in the midst of the historic area. Wanting to cram as much into our trip as possible and being on limited time, we decided to drive that night, after our fancy dinner, to Charlottesville so we could get an early start the next day. It is about a two-hour trip, so it was getting late as we approached Charlottesville. We started looking for a place to stay, at this point pretty exhausted from our full day of sightseeing and our multi-course meal. Unfortunately for us, we did not realize that

Fig 6: Jen at Jefferson's grave at Monticello, 1992 (photo by Amy Poort Jones)

it was freshman orientation week at the University of Virginia. There was not a room to be found in Charlottesville that night.

We slept in the car in a motel parking lot. There was no problem getting an early start that morning. The sun was barely up as we headed to Shoney's for breakfast and a place to brush our teeth. We must have been quite a lovely sight as we arrived for our tour at Monticello. I have proof of that. For some reason, I let Amy take a picture of me standing at Jefferson's grave. I look like I just slept in my car.

A more recent visit to Monticello was with another group of friends from work. Six of us trekked down to Charlottesville for the day to tour Jefferson's home and grounds. It was a beautiful day to stroll around the property, and especially interesting since we were a diverse group— some interested in history and some more interested in nature. I paid more attention than I ever had before to the trees and plants on Jefferson's grounds and have a new appreciation for his vast knowledge and interests. The part I remember most was the visit we made to the Jefferson Winery just up the road. We must have tried half a dozen varieties of wine, and not being a real drinker, I would sip each kind and pour the rest into my friend's glass. Jefferson, a big wine fan, would have been pleased.

Fig 7: Jefferson's grave at Monticello

Much has been written about Jefferson over the years, including by himself. His extensive collection of letters provides a detailed view of eighteenth- and early nineteenth-century Virginia life. He even went so far as to write his own epitaph. Of all his accomplishments and illustrious positions held, Thomas Jefferson wanted to be remembered for three deeds: Author of the Declaration of Independence, Author of the Statute of Religious Freedom for the State of Virginia, and Founder of the University of Virginia.[1]

My project was never intended as a biography of each Declaration signer. The focus of the adventure was finding the graves, so it seems the emphasis here should be on deaths and burials. Not that I am normally a morbid person, but along the way there were so many interesting aspects of the deaths and burials of these men that it became a story unto itself.

Being a big fan of John Adams, the circumstances surrounding the deaths of Thomas Jefferson and John Adams captured my interest years ago. Even today I am still amazed at the incredible coincidence of two great founding fathers dying on the same day, especially two men with such a special bond and checkered past.

As a park ranger at the Thomas Jefferson Memorial in Washington, DC, and previously a seasonal park ranger at the Adams National Historical Park in Quincy, Massachusetts, I often speak of the friendship between Jefferson and Adams. These two men came from different backgrounds, yet worked together for the good of the thirteen colonies in the Continental Congress. Adams realized Jefferson's writing talent and Jefferson's inclusion on the Declaration's drafting committee made history.[2]

---

1   Frederick D. Nichols and James A. Bear, Jr., *Monticello: A Guidebook* (Monticello, VA: Thomas Jefferson Memorial Foundation, 1993), 67.

2   John Ferling, *John Adams: A Life* (New York: Henry Holt and Company, 1992), 147.

Working together for independence in Philadelphia established the friendship. Time in Europe serving as diplomats solidified the friendship,[3] as evidenced by Jefferson and Adams touring the English countryside and visiting Shakespeare's home.[4] Returning to the newly created United States, both men held positions in George Washington's administration. During this time, however, Adams and Jefferson started developing different ideas on how the new nation should run. They were now on different sides. This culminated in the presidential election of 1800 when Adams lost his bid for reelection to Jefferson. What had once been a close friendship deteriorated due to political differences.[5] Yet years later, after both men retired and were able to reflect back on the illustrious events they had been a part of, Jefferson and Adams patched up their friendship and engaged in a unique correspondence. Never again meeting face to face, they relived the glory days, discussed current events, and argued historical and philosophical questions through letters. This began around 1813 when Adams wrote to Jefferson, "You and I, ought not to die, before We have explained ourselves to each other,"[6] and continued until their deaths.

Which brings me back to the whole point here. Even without this convoluted history it would have been an amazing coincidence for these two great patriots to have died on the same day. Add to this coincidence the fact that both men died on July 4, 1826, fifty years to the day that

---

3   Ferling, *John Adams: A Life*, 269.

4   "John Adams" on Monticello.org, accessed on March 4, 2016, https://www.monticello.org/site/jefferson/john-adams.

5   Ferling, *John Adams: A Life*, 316.

6   "John Adams to Thomas Jefferson, 15 July 1813, with Postscript from Abigail Adams to Thomas Jefferson, [ca. 15 July 1813]," Founders Online, National Archives (http://founders.archives.gov/documents/Jefferson/03-06-02-0247 [last update: 2015-12-30]). Source: The Papers of Thomas Jefferson, Retirement Series, vol. 6, 11 March to 27 November 1813, ed. J. Jefferson Looney. Princeton: Princeton University Press, 2009, pp. 296–298.

the Declaration of Independence was approved, a document both played a critical role in creating. Adding still more to this incredible story are John Adams' last words. Supposedly on his deathbed on July 4, he said, "Thomas Jefferson survives."[7] Adams, at age 90 in Quincy, Massachusetts, would have no way of knowing that his friend Jefferson, at age 83, had already died earlier that day at Monticello. With the deaths of these two founding fathers, two of the last links to the Revolutionary era were gone, although one Declaration signer still survived—Charles Carroll.[8]

Jefferson serves as a perfect example of a great man—appreciated in his own lifetime, whom one would expect would be honored in death. His popularity was evidenced by his need for a second home, Poplar Forest, since people regularly stopped in to visit at Monticello, providing no privacy.[9] His financial problems were well documented and soon after his death, Jefferson's descendants sold Monticello.[10] One would expect that despite the change in ownership a family burial ground would be well kept out of respect for the dead. This was not the case at Monticello.

According to Robert Kean, who wrote *History of the Graveyard at Monticello*, respect was not paid to those at rest at Monticello. He wrote of the destruction of the graveyard soon after Jefferson's death. New walls built around the yard did no good. Jefferson's great-granddaughter Ellen Wayles Harrison wrote in 1885 of a new attempt to dissuade disturbers:

---

7   Ferling, *John Adams: A Life*, 444.

8   Dumas Malone, *The Story of the Declaration of Independence* (New York: Oxford University Press, 1954), 96.

9   Natalie S. Bober, *Thomas Jefferson: Man on a Mountain* (New York: Atheneum, 1988), 233.

10 Marc Leepson, *Saving Monticello: The Levy Family's Epic Quest to Rescue the House that Jefferson Built* (New York: The Free Press, 2001), 22.

It was hoped that the grating, affording a full view of the group of Jefferson graves would satisfy the public. This hope was elusive...The locks on the gate were broken as fast as they were renewed. The graveyard was constantly the object of care and attention to the family but to no avail. Turf laid one month would be trodden up the next. One individual, showing a piece of Jefferson's tomb, boasted that he had taken a sledge hammer up from Charlottesville to secure it.[11]

What a commentary on a society that honors its political heroes this way. Never mind heroes; no one should have his headstone chipped away. The government must have felt the same way, for in 1883, Congress gave money for a new headstone for Thomas Jefferson at Monticello.[12]

Apparently there was debate over placement of the old stone, but eventually a location was chosen—Columbia, Missouri. As the first state university created on land from the Louisiana Purchase, the University of Missouri was honored with Jefferson's original headstone. Two significant facets of Jefferson's life were represented here—education and the Louisiana Purchase.[13] It is a shame that Jefferson's headstone had to be moved for preservation purposes.

Thomas Jefferson is one of many of the Declaration signers to have some unusual element associated with his death or burial. In this case both the historic day of his death and the bizarre treatment his grave received serve as a fascinating beginning to this quest of visiting all

11   Robert H. Kean, *History of the Graveyard at Monticello* (Charlottesville, VA: The Thomas Jefferson Memorial Foundation, 1972), 10.
12   Kean, *History of the Graveyard at Monticello*, 15.
13   Kean, *History of the Graveyard at Monticello*, 16.

fifty-six signers' graves. As a child visiting Monticello, who would have guessed that trip would lead to the pages that follow?

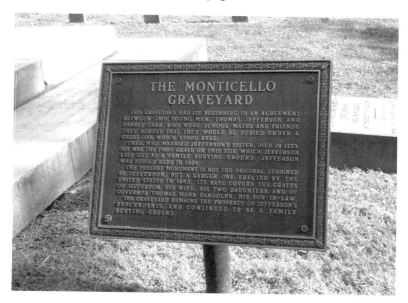

Fig 8: Sign at the Monticello graveyard

III

Road Trip to Richmond

The next grave photograph was also found in my dresser drawer and takes me back to the summer of 1997. As I mentioned already, throughout my travels as a park ranger, I have been lucky to come across people with similar interests. Only someone with a love of history could tolerate all of the trips and stops to old houses or battlefields or graveyards. Most of my tolerant friends will be met throughout this story. I have road tripped with many friends over the years, to many a historic site, but two people will appear most frequently. The first is Bert, whom I met during the summer of 1996, while we were both working at Gettysburg. Summers were fun because there were a lot of young people around who were interested in history. I should have realized Bert was serious about the subject when I saw his car bumper with the sticker, "I Brake For Historical Markers." We did an occasional trip that first summer, such as a day in Baltimore to Fort McHenry and the Inner Harbor, but I got to know Bert better as our careers followed similar paths.

After my summer season in Gettysburg, I was fortunate to get a winter position at Colonial National Historical Park. At the end of that season I returned to Gettysburg for the summer and Bert took the summer seasonal position at Jamestown. Bert enjoys his history and likes traveling to historic sites. Since we lived only a few hours apart, we would meet up occasionally for some sightseeing. One such trip brought us to Richmond, Virginia. We met at Chicka-

Fig 9: St. John's Church, Richmond, Virginia

hominy Bluff, a Civil War battlefield site. I'm sure I was late as usual and Bert was early. He had planned out a number of places to visit—the State Capitol, the Museum of the Confederacy, the Valentine Museum, and St. John's Episcopal Church.

Bert wanted to visit this church, not only because it claims to be Richmond's oldest church, but because it was here in 1775 that Patrick Henry was thought to have uttered those famous words, "give me liberty or give me death."[14] The Royal Governor of Virginia had disbanded the House of Burgesses, the colony's representative assembly, not allowing it to meet in Williamsburg (then Virginia's capital), so the group moved

---

14   Sue Bratt St. Amant, *St. John's Church: A Pictorial History* (Richmond, VA: St. John's Church Foundation, 1996), 10.

its meeting place to Richmond.[15] At the time Bert suggested visiting the church, I don't think I even knew that Henry's famous words were spoken there. I was along for the ride, always up for a new historic adventure.

We toured the church, hearing about the architecture, building history, and events that took place there. Then we walked around the churchyard to investigate the graves. Among the prominent church members buried there was Edgar Allan Poe's mother, Elizabeth Arnold Poe. Apparently her grave was unmarked for years because she had been an actress, which was not considered a respectable career. The marker was placed in 1927;[16] she died in 1813.[17]

Also in the graveyard, near the original east entrance door, George Wythe was buried. I probably recognized him as the law professor who Jefferson studied under and whose house is preserved in Colonial Williamsburg. I snapped a quick picture, thinking it was interesting to find Wythe's grave. Being that I was just along for the ride and didn't really know what to expect at this historic spot, Wythe's grave was a bonus, which came in particularly handy as this project progressed.

George Wythe, as it turns out, is another signer with an interesting death story. A well-respected lawyer and professor in colonial Virginia, Wythe was supposedly poisoned by his great-nephew. I made a return visit to St. John's Church to learn more about Wythe and his grave in November 2002. Three folks working the site were especially friendly and offered a story on Wythe's demise. Supposedly his sister Ann's grandson, and a mulatto boy were named in Wythe's will. The great-nephew was a bit impatient and wanted to get his hands on Wythe's

---

15   Alonzo Thomas Dill, *George Wythe: Teacher of Liberty* (Williamsburg, VA: Virginia Independence Bicentennial Commission, 1979), 27.

16   St. Amant, *St. John's Church*, 43.

17   "Elizabeth Arnold Poe" on findagrave.com, accessed on March 4, 2016, http://findagrave.com/cgi-bin/fg.cgi?page=gr&GRid=4074.

money and was not too fond of sharing with Wythe's local friend. So both Wythe and the mulatto boy were poisoned with arsenic on strawberries in 1806. The mulatto died within a week and Wythe figured out what had happened, so had time to change his will as he lingered for a few weeks. Wythe's loyal housekeeper was also affected, however not as badly, since she had put cream on her strawberries. Ironically, Wythe worked on a law to not allow blacks to testify over whites in court. So the testimony of his housekeeper, a former slave who survived, could not be used in court. It is also ironic, since Wythe was against slavery, that his African-American housekeeper could not testify at the trial and the killer would not be punished. Bruce Chadwick's book, *I Am Murdered: George Wythe, Thomas Jefferson, and the Killing that Shocked a New Nation*, goes into some detail on this tragic event and the court case that followed.[18]

My main reason for returning to Richmond and St. John's Church was to find out if there was any question as to George Wythe's burial spot in the cemetery or if he had been moved at any time. The guides at the church assured me his burial spot was the original. I noticed though, when I looked again at Wythe's headstone, that it said 1922. This begs the question about an original headstone and what might have happened to it. According to *St. John's Church: A Pictorial History*, by Sue Bratt St. Amant, Wythe's grave was unmarked, as noted by a 1901 newspaper article about the cemetery. "Antonio Graffignia, the keeper of St. John's for many decades, had marked the spot from information given to him by a Church Hill resident, Mr. Charles J. Sinton. Mr. Sinton stated that the site of the grave had been shown to him when he was a boy in 1836

---

18   Bruce Chadwick, *I Am Murdered: George Wythe, Thomas Jefferson, and the Killing That Shocked a New Nation* (Hoboken, NJ: John Wiley and Sons, Inc., 2009), 234.

and that the grave was still visible at that time."[19] Plans to mark the grave began in 1915, with the final tombstone dedicated on May 24, 1922, at a cost of $785. A number of organizations worked to get this job done.[20]

The fact that it took so long for Wythe to have a proper headstone is surprising when reading accounts of his funeral. The editor of the *Richmond Enquirer*, a good friend of Wythe and Jefferson, Thomas Ritchie wrote:

> LET THE SOLEMN AND LENGTHENED PROCESSION WHICH ATTENDED HIM TO HIS GRAVE DECLARE THE LOSS WHICH WE HAVE SUSTAINED. KINGS MAY REQUIRE MAUSOLEUMS TO CONSECRATE THEIR MEMORY; SAINTS MAY CLAIM THE PRIVILEGES OF CANONIZATION, BUT THE VENERABLE GEORGE WYTHE NEEDS NO OTHER MONUMENT THAN THE SERVICES RENDERED TO HIS COUNTRY AND THE UNIVERSAL SORROW WHICH THAT COUNTRY SHEDS OVER HIS GRAVE.[21]

Even if people of his generation felt his public service was his legacy, the man deserved a stone to mark his grave.

This story reflects caring individuals who did not want to see Wythe's grave lost to the future. Having visited the gravesites of some signers who were not so fortunate, this is pleasing to see. Groups went out of their way to raise funds and organize to get a proper headstone for a prominent colonial patriot. It still boggles my mind that this took place in 1922, when the man died in 1806. As I mentioned though, compared to some stories that follow, Wythe's grave has a happy ending, if one

---

19   St. Amant, *St. John's Church*, 45.

20   St. Amant, *St. John's Church*, 45.

21   Chadwick, *I Am Murdered*, 22.

can say that. It seems reasonable to assume that he lies where he was originally interred, and that the headstone sits fairly close to that spot. Others definitely cannot say the same.

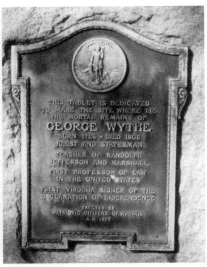

Fig 10: George Wythe's grave, Richmond, Virginia

Fig 11: Close up of the Wythe grave, Richmond, Virginia

IV

To the Plantation

ometime during my winter seasonal job at Colonial, I made
a trip to Berkeley Plantation, along historic Route 5 and the
James River, between Williamsburg and Richmond, Virginia.
This area is known for its old plantation homes belonging
to Virginia's famous families. Many are well-preserved and open to
the public.

Berkeley Plantation was home to generations of the Harrison fam-
ily. William Henry Harrison, the ninth president, was born there.
During the Civil War, Major General George B. McClellan's Union
Army camped there at the end of the Peninsula Campaign of 1862.[22]
Daniel Butterfield, of the Union Army, supposedly composed "Taps"

---

22   Clifford Dowdey, *The Great Plantation: A Profile of Berkeley Hundred and Plantation
     Virginia from Jamestown to Appomattox* (Charles City, VA: Berkeley Plantation, 1988),
     313.

while staying at Berkeley.[23] They claim the Pilgrims did not host the first Thanksgiving; the Virginia settlers did that here too in 1609.[24]

All of this history drew me to visit Berkeley Plantation, but the most relevant history, as far as this story is concerned, is off the main path, beyond the "Taps" Memorial—the family burial ground. On this visit, I snapped a photo of the stone that marked the burial site of Benjamin Harrison V, signer of the Declaration of Independence.

As I continued research into the signers' graves I returned to Berkeley Plantation in August 2005 hoping to get some definitive information on Harrison's grave. For this visit, I went with my friend Michael, who has been on many a grave hunt with me. On this mission I hoped to find out for sure if Harrison was buried in his original location and how it was marked, since the photo I had obviously reflected a recent stone. Since Michael had never visited Berkeley before we decided to take the house tour, not only to thoroughly see the site, but with the hope of gaining information on the grave, burial, or death from the docent. We have both been touring historic sites since we were kids, so we've seen our fair share of tour guides. We've both given tours at historic homes. There is nothing quite like the Southern plantation home tour, with the lady dressed in period clothing (although what period is sometimes in question). And after touring many historic homes, one comes away with many of the same stories, like the origin of "sleep tight and don't let the bed bugs bite." Visitors often hear how beds used to be tightened at night and made of straw as the explanation for this phrase.[25]

23   Dowdey, *The Great Plantation*, 315.

24   Dowdey, *The Great Plantation*, 3.

25   "Mythbuster Friday: Sleep Tight, Don't Let the Bedbugs Bite" on chaddsfordhistorical. wordpress.com, accessed on February 7, 2017, https://chaddsfordhistorical.wordpress. com/2015/07/04/mythbuster-friday-sleep-tight-dont-let-the-bedbugs-bite.

Berkeley, being a plantation, didn't have that particular story but after touring the home we both felt we knew little about its inhabitants and much more about its furnishings. As park rangers, we've been taught over the years to emphasize grander concepts, not just chairs and tables, and to give visitors a sense of the homeowners and who they were. That seemed to be lacking from this tour.

Fig 12: Berkeley Plantation, Charles City, Virginia

As we were exiting the back door (visitors do not get to go upstairs, since the home's owner lives in the house—not a Harrison descendant, but a descendant of the family that bought the home at the turn of the century)[26], I decided to make my move and ask the docent about the Harrison family cemetery. Without getting too deep into the project, I inquired about whether Harrison is really out there, and she gave a smart

---

26   "Berkeley Plantation History" on Berkeleyplantation.com, accessed on February 11, 2017, http://www.berkeleyplantation.com/history.html.

answer about having to ask him. She certainly didn't seem to take my question seriously. I rephrased, explaining how I'd been to other signers' graves and how there are many interesting grave stories out there. Her response was that it would be hard to find Harrison's grave, since there was trouble with vandalism. People coming from the James River would do damage to a Declaration signer's grave. She made it sound like a current problem, that there was no signage out to the family cemetery.

We walked out of the house a bit perplexed by this explanation and feeling like we knew little more than when we'd arrived. We walked around the property down to the river's edge and back toward the cemetery, where just beyond the "Taps" Memorial—clearly marked with arrows, we found the cemetery. Already the docent's story wasn't making sense.

The graveyard was a small area surrounded by a stone wall, with two stone markers within the wall. Neither one was very old. Outside the stone wall was a marker identifying this as the burial site of Benjamin Harrison, the Declaration signer. Also, another stone nearby detailed the difficulties inherent in signing the Declaration. None of these markers appeared old. The gravestone is dated 1972, which leads to the question—do we really know where Harrison's grave is?

Fig 13: Benjamin Harrison's grave, Berkeley Plantation

As we made our way back to the gift shop, we were struck by a missing piece of the story. Nowadays, the slave perspective is a common element at Southern historic sites. Not at Berkeley. No mention of slavery, no slave cabins on the property. The Harrisons would have owned slaves, but the story goes untold at Berkeley. That would make another interesting study. How many of the Declaration signers were slave owners? As folks risking their lives for their independence from Great Britain, how could they deny independence to others? While a great question to consider later, this story is about Harrison's grave.

The idea that graves may not have been marked during the Revolutionary era in order to protect the remains of a prominent patriot does make sense. This was something that came up at another home. Stories are told of the risks faced by those who signed if the Revolution had gone the other way. Berkeley's location along the James, with the British obviously spending time in Virginia and water travel more significant during that period, could make sense. A grave unmarked in the 1790s, when Harrison died, would obviously be hard to identify as time went on, making the recent stones placed in the Berkeley family cemetery the best guess as to Benjamin Harrison's final resting place. I have written to the folks at Berkeley Plantation for clarification, but have not heard back. A return trip to the plantation may be in order to learn more about this grave situation.

Fig 14: Berkeley Plantation Cemetery

V

The First Southern Campaign

My parents planned a big vacation for the summer of 1987. We flew from the East Coast to Seattle, driving down the West Coast to Los Angeles, including a detour to Las Vegas and back to L.A. I'll never forget Dad saying to me at age sixteen, "Well, this will probably be the last family vacation you'll want to go on!"

Fast forward to 1999. Mom and Dad were planning a trip to Charleston, South Carolina, and Savannah, Georgia. We had driven through Savannah on one of our family trips to Florida, but all I remembered was the home of the founder of the Girl Scouts and a cool pirate restaurant. I'd never been to Charleston. What a great historic city that would be to visit. I mentioned to the folks that having never been to Charleston, I'd love to go. So much for kids not wanting to travel with their parents anymore. What an opportunity from my perspective to see some great historic sites, and at very little expense. Not always thinking however, the folks decided to visit these beautiful Southern cities in early August. I'm sure Mom was questioning that decision throughout the trip.

I must have traveled some with the parents since the "last" family vacation to the West Coast, but more recently I had taken to traveling with my history buddies. These friends were used to my frequent picture-taking and occasional stopping to jot down some notes. They shared similar interests in statues or battlefields. I was anxious to explore the squares of Savannah, regardless of the stifling heat and humidity. The friends had also raised my awareness of historic cemeteries and how neat it can be to roam around and try to figure out the stories behind the headstones.

One morning, while Mom slept in, Dad and I got up early so we could walk around historic Savannah before it got too hot. We checked out a bunch of the squares, like Johnson Square with the Nathanael Greene statue. Greene was Washington's trusted general during the Revolution. He served in various northern battles but then moved south to lead the army. The state of Georgia was so thankful for his service that he received a plantation near Savannah. He moved there but died shortly thereafter in 1786. While buried originally in nearby Colonial Park Cemetery, Greene's remains were moved and re-interred under this statue in 1902.[27] Popular generals were also moved from their burial places.

Then Dad and I stumbled over to Colonial Park Cemetery. This was before the signers project began. I liked wandering around old cemeteries and seeing if unexpected well-known people might be found there. Some well-known Southerners rested in this cemetery. One name stood out to Dad and me. As a history major, and knowing my interest in American history, Dad loves to show off his trivia knowledge whenever he can. Don't get him started on John Tyler and his offspring. Tyler lived to age

---

27   "Nathanael Greene Monument" on visit-historic-savannah.com, accessed on May 27, 2017, http://www.visit-historic-savannah.com/nathanael-greene-monument.html.

72, had a child at age 70 with his second wife, Julia, and that child then had a child at age 75. So while John Tyler was president in 1841, he has a grandson still alive today.[28] Dad is amazed by this fact.

After our interest was sparked by the musical *1776*, Dad's favorite question was, whose signature of those that signed the Declaration of Independence is the rarest? The answer is Button Gwinnett of Georgia.[29] Gwinnett was the second signer to die, in May, 1777. Why then doesn't John Morton, the first signer to die, have the rarest signature? Maybe he wrote a lot? Gwinnett died of wounds he suffered in a duel. Well, not only does one find the grave of Button Gwinnett in the Colonial Park Cemetery in Savannah, but across the lawn against a fence is the grave of the person he dueled—Lachlan McIntosh. See what great stories cemeteries can tell. We were so inspired that we got a book at a very nice local bookstore on famous Savannah duels.

That book shed some light on the duel that cost Gwinnett his life. "The duel between McIntosh and Gwinnett was the closing clash between two determined, impetuous, courageous men, both devoted to republican principles, but each also governed by personal impulses and ambitions and little inclined to mediate personal differences when they assumed the nature of a serious affront."[30] Gwinnett and McIntosh were on opposite sides of colonial Georgia politics. Little documentation survives to tell Gwinnett's whole story, and what does exist is slanted by the source, whether from a friend or an enemy of Button Gwinnett's.[31]

---

28   "Genealogy of John Tyler and his Descendants," on sherwoodforest.com/genealogy, accessed on May 31, 2017, http://www.sherwoodforest.org/Genealogy.html.

29   Edwin C. Bridges, Harvey H. Jackson, Kenneth H. Thomas, James H. Young, *Georgia's Signers and the Declaration of Independence* (Atlanta: Cherokee Publishing Company, 1981), 37.

30   Thomas Gamble, *Savannah Duels and Duellists, 1733-1877* (1923; repr., Savannah, GA: The Oglethorpe Press, 1997), 11.

31   Bridges et al., *Georgia's Signers and the Declaration of Independence*, 37.

He came to the colonies from England in search of a better life but struggled with various business ventures, always looking for the next opportunity. He fell into leadership positions in the Georgia government where he angered Lachlan McIntosh by arresting his brother George. The bad blood continued when Lachlan McIntosh was given a military assignment that Gwinnett had wanted, an invasion into Florida that failed miserably, in part because the two men could not work together.[32]

Fellow Georgia signer and friend to Gwinnett, Lyman Hall wrote to Connecticut signer Roger Sherman about the duel:

> HERE IT WAS (IN ASSEMBLY) THAT THE GENL. CALLED HIM (AS 'TIS SAID) A SCOUNDRELL AND LYING RASCAL—I CONFESS I DID NOT HEAR THE WORDS, NOT BEING SO NIGH THE PARTIES. A DUEL WAS THE CONSEQUENCE, IN WHICH THEY WERE PLACED AT 10 OR 12 FOOT DISTANCE. DISCHARGED THEIR PISTOLS NEARLY AT THE SAME TIME. EACH WOUNDED IN THE THIGH. MR. GWINNETT'S THIGH BROKE SO THAT HE FELL—ON WH'H ('TIS SAID) THE GENL. ASKED HIM IF HE CHOSE TO TAKE ANOTHER SHOT—WAS ANSWERED YES, IF THEY WOULD HELP HIM UP (OR WORDS NEARLY THE SAME). THE SECONDS INTERPOSED. MR. GWINNETT WAS BROUGHT IN, THE WEATHER EXTREMELY HOT. A MORTIFICATION CAME ON—HE LANGUISH'D FROM THAT MORNING (FRIDAY) TILL MONDAY MORNING FOLLOWING & EXPIRED. O LIBERTY. WHY DO YOU SUFFER SO MANY OF YOUR FAITHFUL SONS, YOUR WARMEST VOTARIES, TO FALL

---

32   D.J. Drewien, *Button Gwinnett: A Historiography of the Georgia Signer of the Declaration of Independence* (Pittsburgh, PA: RoseDog Books, 2007), 135.

AT YOUR SHRINE. ALAS, MY FRIEND, MY FRIEND.[33]

The duel happened on May 16, 1777, with Gwinnett dying three days later, according to Lyman Hall.[34] The political battles continued, as Gwinnett's supporters argued for McIntosh to suffer consequences for Gwinnett's death. Eventually, McIntosh was sent north and given a role in Washington's army.[35]

I innocently took a picture of Button Gwinnett's grave—his presumed grave anyway—not realizing how important that photo would be to me later. It would turn out to be an early picture in the collection, another photo that would be found in my dresser drawer. It would continue the trend of unusual grave stories.

Fig 15: Button Gwinnett's stone, Colonial Park Cemetery, Savannah, Georgia

When looking at the stone marking Gwinnett's grave, it clearly looks modern, considering the man died in 1777. Almost any source found mentions that Gwinnett is presumed buried in Colonial Park or might be there. It boggles the mind to think a prominent man during his lifetime would go missing after he died. But I would find this situation a lot as I continued the search for the signers.

33   Gamble, *Savannah Duels and Duellists, 1733–1877*, 15.

34   Drewien, *Button Gwinnett: A Historiography*, 181.

35   Drewien, *Button Gwinnett: A Historiography*, 195.

A 1926 Gwinnett biography by Charles Jenkins said this about Gwinnett's burial place:

> IT IS NOT KNOWN WHERE GWINNETT WAS BURIED, NOR HAVE
> WE ANY DETAILS OF HIS FUNERAL SERVICE. AS REV. JAMES
> FOLEY WAS PAID FOR FUNERAL EXPENSES, THE INFERENCE
> IS HE WAS THE OFFICIATING CLERGYMAN. IT IS SUPPOSED
> THAT HIS GRAVE IS IN THE OLD COLONIAL CEMETERY,
> NOW CALLED COLONIAL PARK, WITHIN THE LIMITS OF
> THE CITY OF SAVANNAH. HIS EXECUTOR PROVIDED A
> GRAVESTONE, BUT THIS HAS DISAPPEARED. INDEED, THERE
> IS A NEWSPAPER STORY CURRENT THAT HIS STONE WAS AT
> ONE TIME USED AS THE TOP OF A BAR IN A GROG SHOP IN
> SAVANNAH.[36]

The February 1966 issue of *American Heritage* has a fascinating article, titled "Who's Got Button's Bones?" by Roger M. Williams. The article recounts the work of a retired Savannah school principal Arthur J. Funk, who was inspired to find out more about Gwinnett after visiting the National Archives and seeing a mural with a number of the Declaration signers represented. When asked why Gwinnett was not among them, Funk was told that no one knew what Button Gwinnet looked like. Funk went back to Savannah to begin research. While he did not find a portrait, he may have found something better.

Funk found Gwinnett's will, which led him to believe that Gwinnett's body must have been buried in what is today Colonial Park Cemetery. "I went to looking," recalls Funk, "and I found him seven paces from Archibald Bulloch, the first president [of Georgia]. I found a brown

---

36   Drewien, *Button Gwinnett: A Historiography*, 210.

stub of stone, broken off at ground level. I got the park department's permission, and I started pawing at that stub and poking it with a steel rod."[37] He found what he thought looked like a G or a C and a T and a 7, which he thought must be from Gwinnett and the year he died, 1777. He wanted an archaeologist to dig up the body and try to prove that it was Gwinnett. Knowing that Gwinnett died after being shot in the leg, Funk thought this should be fairly easy to substantiate.

An archaeologist came to examine the remains. The skeleton appeared to be that of a man five feet, six and one-half inches tall. While not well-preserved, the archaeologist did find a little light-colored hair under the skull, and more importantly, damaged bone just above the left knee. Funk was convinced he had found the remains of Button Gwinnett, since Gwinnett's mortal injury was to his left leg.

Not everyone was so sure. Savannah doctor A.J. Waring did not think the evidence was conclusive. The damaged leg bone was sent to the Smithsonian Institution to confirm that a pistol ball could have caused the leg injury. The report concluded that the bone probably was not Gwinnett's, but rather that of a woman, not nearly as tall as originally thought. The damage to the bone likely happened after its burial, not while the person was alive. Smithsonian archaeologist Marshall Newman wrote, "it is highly unlikely, if not fully impossible, for this bone to be that of Button Gwinnett."[38]

Funk was unhappy with these results and felt Newman based his decision on only some of the evidence, disregarding the hair found or the letters visible on the gravestone. Funk asked the mayor for a further investigation. The local historic commission issued a report in September 1959 concluding that Colonial Park Cemetery was where Gwinnett was

---

37   Roger M. Williams, "Who's Got Button's Bones?" *American Heritage*, February 1966.
38   Williams, *American Heritage*, February 1966.

buried and the remains found were probably Button Gwinnett. Waring continued to disagree, saying there was no evidence to prove the claim and insisting the remains looked like a woman's skeleton. Believe it or not, I would hear again on this search that a signer's grave probably held the remains of a woman.

Arthur Funk eventually served in the state legislature. Some people thought he did so in order to get funding for a memorial to Gwinnett, but Funk denied that he created the bill or even voted for it. Five thousand dollars was approved by both houses for a monument to Button Gwinnett. Senator Spence Grayson, speaking in support of this bill, said, "I want to get these bones out of Arthur Funk's living room." Grayson misspoke. The bones were not in the living room, but the guest room. Funk worried about what would happen to the remains after they were exhumed in December 1957. He put them in a new oak coffin in his guest room for five and a half years. He said no guests ever stayed there. "It was talked about as a hush-hush thing," Funk said. "People said, 'he's got the bones in his garage, and he won't let anybody see them! That was ridiculous. They were in the guest room, and nobody ever asked to see them.'"[39]

If the bones were indeed Button Gwinnett's, he got his proper ceremony on October 19, 1964. Two hundred and fifty people gathered at Colonial Park Cemetery to see the new 15-foot-high marble monument created in Gwinnett's honor. Members of various colonial organizations were present. One speaker joked, "We no longer need to ask, 'Button, Button, who has the Button?' Button has been found." Funk was on hand to unveil the plaque, identifying the grave of "Button Gwinnett… whose remains, buried in this cemetery, are believed to be entombed hereunder."[40]

---

39   Williams, *American Heritage*, February 1966.
40   Williams, *American Heritage*, February 1966.

That language does not sound so conclusive, as marking the definitive final resting place for Button Gwinnett. I have recently been in touch with some Georgia historians who do not believe Funk discovered Gwinnett's remains. The belief is that yes, Gwinnett was originally buried in the Colonial Park Cemetery, but that over time the exact location was lost. In 1848 Georgia wanted to bury all of its Declaration signers together, a story we will get to later, and at that time, Gwinnett could not be found.[41] Funk's find is controversial, with answers still not confirmed.

Button Gwinnett's remains may never be properly identified. As far as my search is concerned, the grave in Colonial Park Cemetery is the best option. Even if the reburied remains are not Gwinnett, most likely he was buried in this cemetery after his 1777 death. Thomas Gamble's book, *Savannah's Duels and Duellists, 1733-1877*, claims Colonial Park was the only cemetery in Savannah at the time of the duel and that it was unlikely Gwinnett's body was moved to another town.[42] The elaborate story of these remains shows the interest in the founding fathers, yet also how thoughts or practices on burials have changed over time. Most people today take great care with the headstones of loved ones. Imagine losing track of where someone is buried. This is not the first time this scenario will play out in the search for the signers. These men were the most prominent in their colonies when alive, yet many would suffer very different fates in death.

---

41   Williams, *American Heritage*, February 1966.

42   Gamble, *Savannah Duels and Duellists, 1733–1877*, 23.

VI

The Massachusetts Campaign: Where It All Began

By 1999, I was working in Washington, DC. My friend Michael was also in the city and Bert was working in South Carolina. A new tradition had begun in 1997 of taking historical road trips—first some long weekends, then in 1998, a week-long trip to Tennessee, mostly visiting Civil War battlefields. The choice for the fall 1999 campaign was Boston. Growing up in Connecticut, I could really appreciate a New England autumn. Boston offers plenty of history to explore. As park rangers, we always like to visit other national parks and that obsessive trait kicks in with the national park passport book. It is a little blue book sold at parks. Each time someone visits a national park, they can get the cancellation stamp with the date of their visit.

As rangers we run into serious passport stamp collectors all the time. As one myself, I can appreciate those willing to detour off the road in search of a new stamp and park experience. This passport program is such a great idea.

In October, we were off to Boston. I was particularly excited to show Michael and Bert the homes of John Adams and his family. This was where I spent my first summer as a seasonal in the National Park Service, and as a huge John Adams fan, I love visiting the Old House. All of the items in the house belonged to some member of the family, as the house was passed down through four generations.[43] Working at the Adams house as my first job, I used to say I could retire at age twenty-two, having already had my dream job!

While we endured some frustration maneuvering the South Shore's highway system, we thoroughly enjoyed our tours at the Adams National Historical Park. One can visit the Old House, as well as the birthplaces of the two presidents (two salt box homes, side by side), now surrounded by modern day Quincy. Adams was born in one house. After he married Abigail they moved next door to the home where John Quincy, their son, was born. It was from this house that Abigail would take her young son to hear the sounds of the Battle of Bunker Hill from nearby Penn's Hill.[44]

From birth to death, the whole Adams story is covered at this national park. The year I worked there, in 1993, the park opened a new visitor center, so a ranger stationed there might spend some of the day at the United First Parish Church on the next block. Here in the basement, in a crypt, are the remains of John and Abigail, their son John Quincy, and his wife, Louisa Catherine. This is one grave that we know was moved. John and Abigail were originally buried in the Hancock Cemetery across the street from where they rest today, along with many members of

---

43　"Collections' on nps.gov/adam/learn/historyculture/collections.htm, accessed on January 24, 2019, www.nps.gov/adam/learn/historyculture/collections.htm.

44　David McCullough, *John Adams* (New York: Simon & Schuster, 2001), 22.

Fig 16: Adams plot in Hancock Cemetery, Quincy, Massachusetts

the family and prominent Quincy, Massachusetts, citizens.[45] Designed by Alexander Parris, the church was built from 1827-1828, with John and Abigail's remains moved to a crypt in the basement in 1828.[46]

As mentioned during the Jefferson chapter, but so amazing it is worth repeating, John Adams and Thomas Jefferson both died on the same day, July 4, 1826, fifty years after the adoption of the Declaration of Independence. When visiting the Old House, guests pass by John's magnificent study, the room Abigail added to the home while he finished his presidency. There, in the corner, is where he died that July 4, on the anniversary celebrating the document and the ideal he worked so hard to achieve. In a letter he wrote home to Abigail during that summer of 1776, he described how he thought this momentous event would be remembered:

---

45   "Hancock Cemetery Brochure" on www.discoverquincy.com, accessed on January 24, 2019, https://www.discoverquincy.com/sites/default/files/HancockCemeteryBrochure_web.pdf.

46   "United First Parish Church History," on ufpc.org/ufpc-history, accessed on January 24, 2019, ufpc.org/ufpc-history.

THE SECOND DAY OF JULY 1776, WILL BE THE MOST
MEMORABLE EPOCHA, IN THE HISTORY OF AMERICA. I
AM APT TO BELIEVE THAT IT WILL BE CELEBRATED, BY
SUCCEEDING GENERATIONS, AS THE GREAT ANNIVERSARY
FESTIVAL. IT OUGHT TO BE COMMEMORATED, AS THE DAY
OF DELIVERANCE BY SOLEMN ACTS OF DEVOTION TO GOD
ALMIGHTY. IT OUGHT TO BE SOLEMNIZED WITH POMP AND
PARADE, WITH SHEWS, GAMES, SPORTS, GUNS, BELLS,
BONFIRES AND ILLUMINATIONS FROM ONE END OF THIS
CONTINENT TO THE OTHER FROM THIS TIME FORWARD
FOREVER MORE.[47]

He may have had the date wrong, but John Adams was not too far off
from how Independence Day has come to be celebrated. In 1826 he was
asked by Quincy leaders for a toast to be read on July 4. Adams said, "I
will give you, Independence forever!" When asked if he wanted to say
anything else, he said, "Not a word."[48]

So obviously I would have communed in the crypt with John during
my shifts working the church during that summer, but my favorite picture
is from the Massachusetts campaign of 1999 when my friends captured
a nice photo of me at John's grave. I liked it so much that when I bought
a cute frame to give my future husband, I included the picture of me at
John's grave. It still sits on his desk today. How romantic.

---

47   "Letter from John Adams to Abigail Adams, 3 July 1776," on Massachusetts Historical
      Society, accessed on January 23, 2019, https://www.masshist.org/digitaladams/archive/
      doc?id=L17760703jasecond.

48   McCullough, *John Adams*, 645.

Fig 17: Jen at John and Abigail Adams' graves, United First Parish Church,
Quincy, Massachusetts (photo by Michael Kelly)

It was during this fall trip to Boston that the grave hunt officially began for me. One day we spent doing the Freedom Trail, the miles-long walk around historic Boston. One literally follows the red line painted on the sidewalk to find all the great historic sites in the city. We did the whole thing. Our pictures at the Old North Church show the moon in the background. We had such a fun time, although I'm sure I wasn't so pleasant after we climbed to the top of the Bunker Hill Monument. I hate heights and climbing. We feared for Michael's life when he insisted on getting an accurate photo of the Boston Massacre site, even if it meant standing in the midst of Boston traffic.

But the life-changing event for me would be our visit to the Old Granary Burying Ground, a great old cemetery right along the Freedom Trail. For as long as I can remember, I've been a real picture-taker, and I can remember snapping so many shots of all the famous people buried in that yard—Sam Adams, John Hancock, Paul Revere, Crispus Attucks, and Benjamin Franklin's parents.[49]

While walking along one wall there is a marker to Robert Treat Paine, signer of the Declaration of Independence. His was not a name that rolls off the tongue, like John Hancock or Sam Adams, but a light bulb must have gone off—here in one graveyard are three signers of the Declaration of Independence. One was the man who signed first and in big letters, so that King George supposedly could read it, although there is little evidence to prove that comment.[50]

The light bulb may have gone off, but it didn't stay on too long. When it came to this ultimate final product I should have asked some more questions while there, but who knew then that this big project would come about. I have a vague memory of a sign at the Old Granary Burying Ground implying that time wasn't good to the place and that maybe the headstones don't mark where the bodies actually are—this would eventually become a common theme. How could these men, who risked their lives by attaching their names to a document, be so terribly treated in death? Was it a different attitude toward death in the late eighteenth- and early nineteenth-century? Was it fear of the British during the Revolutionary era? Was it the failure of future generations to properly care for their history, in this case, the graves of heroic ancestors? How many cemeteries have broken headstones or unmowed grass? Thankfully, there are plenty more signers' stories to investigate in order to hopefully address these questions.

Before we leave Boston, however, there are still some interesting stories to explore. Three Declaration signers are buried in one graveyard,

---

49   Charles Chauncey Wells and Suzanne Austin Wells, *Preachers, Patriots & Plain Folks: Boston's Burying Ground Guide to King's Chapel, Granary and Central Cemeteries* (Oak Park, IL: Chauncey Park Press, 2004), 76.

50   Harlow Giles Unger, *John Hancock: Merchant King and American Patriot* (Edison, NJ: Castle Books, 2005), 241.

along with a number of other historic people. One might think such a famous yard would be well-documented and clearly identify where people were buried. Old Granary was first used as a cemetery in 1660, the land at one time being part of Boston Common. Old Granary got its name from a large grain storage building in the 1730s that provided food for the poor. The building did not last, but the name stuck to the cemetery.[51] According to CityofBoston.gov, the cemetery has about 2,345 gravestones, yet probably about 5,000 people buried there.[52] Folks did not always mark graves with a headstone, so that accounts for some of the confusion. Time can take a toll on a place like this too. Drainage and flooding have been a problem. Cows even grazed among the stones in the early days of the cemetery.[53]

Construction nearby also accounted for some damaged stones. A quote found on the CityofBoston.gov webpage also sheds some light on this situation. "The gravestones' original haphazard configuration was rearranged into straighter rows over the years to accommodate both nineteenth-century aesthetics and the modern lawnmower."[54] It strikes me as strange that headstones were moved and actual burial spots are unknown for the purpose of aesthetics and lawnmowers. This is certainly a more complex situation than I understand, but I guess I assumed when people were laid to rest, they really were laid to rest. While Granary is a fascinating place to wander through today and provides a great sense of

---

51   Wells and Wells, *Preachers, Patriots & Plain Folks*, 76.

52   "Granary Burying Ground" on www.boston.gov/cemeteries/granary-burying-ground, accessed on January 24, 2019, https://www.boston.gov/cemeteries/granary-burying-ground.

53   Wells and Wells, *Preachers, Patriots & Plain Folks*, 78.

54   "Granary Burying Ground" on www.boston.gov/cemeteries/granary-burying-ground, accessed on January 24, 2019, https://www.boston.gov/cemeteries/granary-burying-ground.

history, I can't help but wonder about those whose stones do not match where their bodies lie or those that do not even have stones at all.

Sorting out the Granary Burying Ground story has been challenging. It is almost like a game of musical chairs, wondering if the headstone marks where the remains rest. This seemed like a riddle that might never be solved. Oliver Wendell Holmes noticed this too. "Epitaphs were never famous for truth, but the old reproach of 'Here lies' never had such a wholesale illustration as in these outraged burial places, where the stone does lie above and the bones do not lie beneath."[55]

I'm intrigued by Robert Treat Paine's situation, because his marker in the cemetery is found on a wall. Does that mean he was buried in that part of the cemetery, or was that a convenient space to put up a marker? I have yet to figure out that part of the story. Recently though, I came across a reference in a 1902 guide to Old Granary that mentioned, "a headstone of notable patriotic significance, as that of a famous signer of the Declaration of Independence, is one bearing the simple inscription:

No. 88

The tomb of R.T. Paine

1810[56]

Every time I find something new about a grave, it leads to more questions. I would guess that the 1810 stone disappeared over time, especially with what has been written about the cemetery over the years, and the marker on the wall currently replaced the old stone. Another unexplained mystery is why the year 1810 is listed on this source, when Paine died

---

55   Susan Wilson, *Boston Sites and Insights: An Essential Guide to Historic Landmarks In and Around Boston* (Boston, MA: Beacon Press, 2003), 95.

56   Boston, Mass. Cemetery Dept, *Historical Sketch and Matters Appertaining to the Granary Burialground* (Boston: Boston Municipal Printing Office, 1902), 21.

in 1814. Maybe I will return to Boston someday to discover the details of this story.

I am also intrigued about why some signers are more remembered than others. Robert Treat Paine died in 1814, living a long life after signing the Declaration. Yet little is known of him. The above reference in 1902 called Paine a famous signer, maybe in local Massachusetts circles. Paine served as a lawyer for the prosecution of the British soldiers involved in the Boston Massacre against fellow lawyer John Adams. He served in the Continental Congress, was the first attorney general of Massachusetts, and then served as a judge.[57] As someone who has always been interested in history, I'm surprised how little I know about him.

While not wanting to write biographies here, I do want to share one more item I found interesting about Paine in his diary—how he documented his claim to fame, the Declaration of Independence. According to the Massachusetts Historical Society, who have a large collection of Robert Treat Paine's papers, this is his diary for early July 1776:

(July) 2—Rain'd hard coold the air much

3—Cool day

4—Cool the Independence of the States voted & declared

5—Hott—[58]

I love how he recorded just another day in his life and American history. Another benefit of this grave hunt has been the neat historical

---

57   "Robert Treat Paine diary, July 1776" on Massachusetts Historical Society, accessed January 24, 2019, https://www.masshist.org/database/viewer.php?item_id=3364&pid=3.

58   "Robert Treat Paine diary, July 1776" on Massachusetts Historical Society, accessed January 24, 2019, https://www.masshist.org/database/viewer.php?item_id=3364&img_step=1&pid=3&mode=transcript#page1.

characters I have met along the way. Maybe this will inspire others to take an interest in some of the lesser-known figures in history. Now back to the Old Granary Burying Ground and two of the more well-known leaders of the American Revolution.

Fig 18: Robert Treat Paine's stone, Old Granary Burying Ground, Boston, Massachusetts

Both Sam Adams and John Hancock had funerals with processions that led to Old Granary. According to biographies, neither man had a stone to mark a burial site for many many years. An 1885 biography of Adams claims "his dust lies almost beneath the feet of the passers in the great thoroughfare, and no stone marks the spot."[59] Thousands of people participated in John Hancock's funeral in 1793. An article in the *Boston Daily Globe* on the hundredth anniversary of Hancock's death includes

---

59   James Kendall Hosmer, *Samuel Adams* (Boston, MA: Houghton Mifflin Company, 1885), 417.

the headline, "First Signer of Freedom's Roll, Yet He Has no Fitting Monument."[60] The article describes a large floral arrangement that was left on his grave in honor of the hundredth anniversary of the day he died, then continues, "Yet he who was buried with pomp and display lies in a neglected grave, marked only by a dilapidated stone, upon whose surface can barely be traced the inscription, No. 16 Tomb of Hancock."[61]

The situation may have been worse than an unmarked grave for John Hancock. Legend has it that shortly after his burial grave robbers wanted the fancy jewelry he was buried with. When they couldn't get the rings off his fingers, they just cut off his hands.[62] Imagine having the famous hand that had signed the Declaration of Independence. While documentation on this morbid story is sketchy, it certainly adds to the bizarre death and burial incidents surrounding the Declaration signers.

Ironically John Hancock, as president of the Continental Congress and first to sign the Declaration, has more than his share of unbelievable burial-related stories. An 1886 *Bacon's Dictionary of Boston* by Edwin Monroe Bacon, mentioned the slab with the simple inscription that one time marked Hancock's grave at Old Granary. He cites an account from 1882, describing the building of a store on Park Street that bordered the cemetery. The burial ground wall came down and a new one was built to improve lighting in the building's basement. Apparently several tombstones had been used in the old wall, including Hancock's, so when rebuilt, those stones were laid aside to be thrown out or reused in the burial ground. The source claimed Hancock's stone at the time might still be there, but was not near his actual grave. Just when you think it can't get any worse, it does.

---

60   "No 16 Tomb of Hancock," *Boston Daily Globe*, October 9, 1893, p. 8.

61   "No 16 Tomb of Hancock," *Boston Daily Globe*, October 9, 1893, p. 8.

62   Wilson, *Boston Sites and Insights*, 97.

IN TEARING DOWN THE OLD WALL, THE TOMB OF JOHN
HANCOCK MUST HAVE BEEN BROKEN INTO, AS THE WALL
FORMED ONE SIDE OF IT, SO THERE IS NO PROOF THAT EVEN
HIS BODY REMAINS THERE. THE BODY WAS ENCLOSED IN
A LEAD COFFIN: WHO KNOWS BUT THIS MAY HAVE BEEN
CONVERTED INTO WATER- PIPES, OR USED UP IN VARIOUS
PLUMBING OPERATIONS?[63]

Finally, in February 1894, the Massachusetts legislature agreed to spend up to $3,000 "for the purpose of erecting a suitable memorial over the grave of Governor John Hancock."[64] A formal dedication took place on September 10, 1896. Since both of Hancock's children died in early childhood and there were no direct descendants, a great grand-niece, Mary Elizabeth Wood unveiled the new monument. Massachusetts Governor Roger Wolcott spoke on behalf of the Commonwealth:

IT HAS LONG BEEN A MATTER OF COMMENT, AND POSSIBLY OF
REGRET TO THE COMMONWEALTH OF MASSACHUSETTS,
THAT THE GRAVE OF HER FIRST GOVERNOR, A MAN WHO
PLAYED SO LARGE A PART IN THE REVOLUTIONARY PERIOD,
REMAINED IN THE HEART OF THE PRINCIPAL CITY OF
THE COMMONWEALTH UNMARKED BY ANY ENDURING
MONUMENT.[65]

---

63   Edwin Monroe Bacon, *Bacon's Dictionary of Boston* (Boston, MA: Houghton, Mifflin and Company, 1886), 279.

64   Abram English Brown, *John Hancock: His Book* (Boston, MA: Lee and Shepard Publishers, 1898), 245.

65   Brown, *John Hancock: His Book*, 245.

THIS MONUMENT WILL BE ONE OF THOSE SPOTS TO WHICH THE FEET OF PILGRIMS WILL BE DIRECTED. IT WILL BE ONE OF THE MEMORIES WHICH THOSE WHO VISIT US FROM OTHER STATES OR OTHER COUNTRIES WILL BEAR AWAY WITH THEM FROM HISTORIC BOSTON AND HISTORIC MASSACHUSETTS, AND AS THE HURRYING CROWD PASSES BY THE SIDEWALK, I HOPE THAT IT WILL SPEAK ELOQUENTLY FOR ALL YEARS TO COME OF PATRIOTIC AND LOYAL SERVICE TO THE COMMONWEALTH.[66]

Fig 19 and 20: John Hancock's grave, Old Granary Burying Ground, Boston, Massachusetts

A similar situation pertained to the remains of Sam Adams in 1898, when his grave was finally marked by the Massachusetts Society of the

---

66   Brown, *John Hancock: His Book*, 246.

Sons of the Revolution. Major Frank Briggs, president of the organization, spoke at the ceremony:

> ONE HUNDRED AND TWENTY-THREE YEARS AGO ON THIS VERY DAY, IN COMPANY WITH JOHN HANCOCK, SAMUEL ADAMS LEFT LEXINGTON AS THE BRITISH TROOPS WERE HEARD APPROACHING THAT TOWN. THE HOUR OF RESISTANCE HAD COME, AND HE EXCLAIMED TO HANCOCK, "WHAT A GLORIOUS MORNING IS THIS." HISTORIANS AND COMMENTATORS HAVE MANY TIMES CRITICIZED THE FACT THAT NO SUITABLE MONUMENT MARKED HIS LAST RESTING PLACE. WE, THE SONS OF THE REVOLUTION, BELIEVING THAT IT IS OUR DUTY TO PLACE BEFORE THE PEOPLE A SUITABLE MEMORIAL OF HIS DEEDS, AND IN FURTHERANCE OF OUR CHARTER TO KEEP ALIVE THE SPIRIT OF PATRIOTISM AMONG ALL MEN, TRANSFER TO THE CITY THIS RUGGED BOWLDER.[67]

Before placing the rock over Adams' grave the tomb was opened on March 26, 1898, "for purposes of identification, though it was well-known that Samuel Adams was buried in the Checkley Tomb, the property of his wife…The tomb was found to be in excellent condition, perfectly intact, constructed solidly of brick throughout, the roof being slightly curved. Every indication furnished satisfactory evidence and left no doubt, if any existed, that the great organizer of the Revolution was

---

67　"Left in Its Natural State. Immense Bowlder Marks the Resting Place of Samuel Adams in Old Granary Burying Ground," *Boston Daily Globe*, April 20, 1898, 6.

laid to rest in the Checkley tomb."[68] Even in 1898, there seemed some question about whether the famous signer was really buried there.

Fig 21: Samuel Adams' grave, Old Granary Burying Ground, Boston, Massachusetts

Patriots from Massachusetts played a huge role in the American Revolution and were popular amongst their fellow citizens. With that in mind, it seems incredible that these founding fathers would suffer such fates in death. For a commonwealth aware and proud of its history, it is surprising to think that John Hancock's remains could end up in a nearby construction project. The man who signed his name in big letters, proudly declaring independence from Great Britain, does not literally rest in peace. While a visit to the Old Granary Burying Ground provides a strong sense of history, walking along the paths through the old tombstones now also stirs up more questions about the fate of those buried there. My search for the signers began when visiting this old cemetery. I could never have imagined then the unusual stories and history I would discover along this journey.

68   Boston, Mass. Cemetery Dept, *Historical Sketch and Matters Appertaining to the Granary Burialground* (Boston: Boston Municipal Printing Office, 1902), 17.

VII

Close to Home: Part One

I arrived in Washington, DC, in the summer of 1998. A number of new park rangers were also hired around the same time and many of us came to Washington because the Mall is a big park with high turnover and a chance to get permanent government status. Some people work years as seasonal park rangers, spending six months at a time at a park, hoping to one day get a permanent job. I spent about five years working seasonally and consider myself pretty lucky to have had the experiences I had. One good friend I made at the Mall was Ernie, who had a similar story to mine, in that we had traveled the seasonal circuit for a while and were looking to finally get permanent status. Ernie and I had common days off and bonded over baseball, taking in a lot of major and minor league games. I always remember Ernie saying that he didn't plan on staying in DC too long (and he didn't), so he wanted to see as much of the city's attractions as possible before leaving. We spent a lot of our weekends, which meant Tuesdays and Wednesdays, touring local museums and historic sites. Over twenty years later and I still pass places that I remember visiting with Ernie that first summer.

When new to an area, people rely on the locals to help show them around. James was relatively new to the park too, but had grown up around DC. Ernie and I took advantage of James' knowledge of the area to fulfill the mission of seeing the local attractions. I remember James taking us to Glen Echo Park, the Clara Barton House, and Rock Creek Park. For as much traveling as I did with Ernie, he almost did not make it into this book, but if readers hang on toward the end, Ernie and his wife will make a rather entertaining appearance later on in the signer story.

For some reason, Ernie did not partake of our weekday trip to Congressional Cemetery in February 2000, but motivated to see the local sites, James served as tour guide for me and another ranger, Scott. Congressional Cemetery in Washington, DC, was founded in 1807 and was the final resting place for many famous Washingtonians.[69] As its name implies, many members of Congress also were laid to rest here, in some cases, not permanently. Some, like John Quincy Adams, who died in the Capitol building, would rest here temporarily before returning to a home state like Massachusetts. Since I just mentioned Ernie, I should say that a great DC adventure we had was touring the Capitol and visiting the room where John Quincy Adams died. I was so excited, being a big Adams fan, to get this behind-the-scenes tour. I took my picture sitting proudly on the couch where I was told John Quincy died. The couch has thankfully been reupholstered. As we left, the guide said that maybe JQ had died on the other couch in the room. It was too late to get my picture on the other couch. Oh well.

---

69   "Congressional Cemetery Introductory Tour," on congressionalcemetery.org, accessed on January 24, 2019, https://www.congressionalcemetery.org/pdf/Walking-Tours/Intro%20Tour.pdf.

Other members of Congress would never be buried at Congressional Cemetery, but would still be remembered with a monument there. Cenotaphs, which literally means "empty tomb," were made of local sandstone to honor members of Congress who died while in office. According to the Congressional Cemetery tour brochure, "This practice ended around 1870 when Congressman Hoar claimed the sight of these cenotaphs gave new meaning to the horror of death." Though many are empty tombs, about 80 Congressmen are buried under their cenotaphs, out of 165 total in the cemetery.[70]

Of particular interest to me on the trip to Congressional Cemetery was not J. Edgar Hoover, director of the FBI, or Robert Mills, designer of the Washington Monument. Nor was it finding Mathew Brady, Civil War photographer, or John Philip Sousa, composer of marches and conductor of the Marine Band. I was most interested in finding Elbridge Gerry, signer of the Declaration of Independence from Massachusetts.[71] James took us to pay our respects to Gerry, who is buried on the north side of the cemetery. At a time when most stones were simple sandstone, Gerry's elaborate marker was made of Massachusetts marble. Gerry died in 1814, but Congress put the stone up in 1823.[72] At the time of his death, Gerry was serving as vice president under James Madison.

Elbridge Gerry viewed the signing of the Declaration as "the greatest single act of his entire life."[73] John Adams admired his dedication to

---

70 "Congressional Cemetery Introductory Tour," on congressionalcemetery.org, accessed on January 24, 2019, https://www.congressionalcemetery.org/pdf/Walking-Tours/Intro%20Tour.pdf.

71 "Congressional Cemetery Introductory Tour," on congressionalcemetery.org, accessed on January 24, 2019, https://www.congressionalcemetery.org/pdf/Walking-Tours/Intro%20Tour.pdf.

72 "Monument of Elbridge Gerry completed," *Columbian Centinel*, Boston, MA, August 2, 1823, accessed on June 2, 2019, http://www.rarenewspapers.com/view/557560.

73 George Athan Billias, *Elbridge Gerry, Founding Father and Republican Statesman* (New York: McGraw-Hill Book Company, 1976), 1-7.

independence, saying, "If every Man here was a Gerry, the Liberties of America would be safe against the Gates of Earth and Hell."[74] Yet there were other memorable moments in his career. Gerry participated in the Constitutional Convention, supporting the work at first, but ultimately deciding not to sign the document since it originally lacked a Bill of Rights. He served in the U.S. House of Representatives, as a diplomat to France, and as governor of Massachusetts.[75]

While Gerry was not the most popular politician—he was known for often changing his mind, not having a sense of humor, and being a snob—he was dedicated to his work for the country.[76] The quote on his grave says, "It is the duty of every man, though he may have but one day to live, to devote that day to the good of his country."[77] Perhaps the term most associated with Gerry is the word gerrymandering, which came about from his time as governor. He rearranged some voting districts to benefit his party, so the opposing press made cartoon maps to make that area look like a salamander. Gerrymander has stuck to mean a funny-shaped district that is created to help a particular party.[78]

Congressional Cemetery's webpage has a lot of interesting history posted, including articles from Washington, DC's newspaper, the *National Intelligencer*, covering Gerry's death in November 1814:

---

74   Billias, *Elbridge Gerry, Founding Father and Republican Statesman*, 70.

75   Mark O. Hatfield, with the Senate Historical Office, *Vice Presidents of the United States, 1789-1993* (Washington, DC: U.S. Government Printing Office, 1997), 63-68.

76   John and Katherine Bakeless, *Signers of the Declaration* (Boston, MA: Houghton Mifflin Company, 1969), 63.

77   Hatfield, *Vice Presidents of the United States*, 1789-1993, 63.

78   Hatfield, *Vice Presidents of the United States*, 1789-1993, 63.

This day we have a melancholy duty to perform. Another of the Worthies of the Revolution, the tried Patriot and consistent Politician, the second Officer of our Government, the venerable Gerry, is no more! Yesterday, between the hours of ten and eleven, he breathed his last. His death was as sudden as it was unexpected. In apparent health he presided in the Senate during an arduous sitting on the preceding day; fifteen minutes before his death, although in his seventieth year, he bade fair to outlive many of those who read these lines. At a few minutes warning, the thread of life was cut, and his spirit winged its flight to happier realms.[79]

The newspaper goes on to describe his death. He had gone out to take care of some business and returned home because he didn't feel well. "Being placed again in the carriage, he was reconveyed to his lodgings. On the arrival of the carriage there, he was found to be insensible, and expired immediately after, almost without a groan or sigh."[80]

The details of Gerry's funeral were also covered in the paper, listing who participated in the service and the procession leading to the burial. From all indications, Gerry is one signer who remained in his original burial location.

Over the course of this search for the signers I have seen some pretty shabby cemeteries, as far as broken headstones or unmowed grass.

---

79 *The National Intelligencer*, Thursday, November 24, 1814, on bytesofhistory.com/ Cemeteries, accessed on January 24, 2019, http://bytesofhistory.org/Cemeteries/ DC_Congressional/Obits/G/G_PDF/Gerry_Elbridge.pdf.

80 The *National Intelligencer*, Thursday, November 24, 1814, on bytesofhistory.com/ Cemeteries, accessed on January 24, 2019, http://bytesofhistory.org/Cemeteries/ DC_Congressional/Obits/G/G_PDF/Gerry_Elbridge.pdf.

Another interesting element of the story here is the situation with Congressional Cemetery. Visiting the website, and having toured the cemetery on days with special tours taking place, there is an obvious sense of pride in this cemetery's history. Yet a big part of what has kept this old cemetery in good shape is the locals, who use these historic grounds for walking their dogs. Never having had pets, I was originally appalled at the idea of using a historic cemetery as a place for dogs to roam around. But upon learning about this further, I've come to see that if it weren't for these dog walkers taking an interest in this special ground, conditions here could have deteriorated to a point where many of these famous peoples' stones would not be recognizable. Because of the interest of dog owners in the neighborhood, the cemetery has a strong base of volunteers to help care for the grounds, donations to help keep up appearances, and unofficial patrols to help discourage those who might want to vandalize the cemetery. It is a winning situation for all—dog owners who have a special place to walk their pets, and a historic site that will be preserved for future generations.

Fig 22: Elbridge Gerry's grave, Congressional Cemetery,
Washington, DC

VIII

Connecticut: Round One

I was well situated in Washington, DC, working on the National Mall and living in Arlington, Virginia in 1999, when the phone rang one day. The person on the phone was calling to find out about my job with the National Park Service. It turns out that we had met as children when our fathers, both educators in Connecticut, worked together. Our parents had recently met for dinner, sharing stories about their children. Jonathan had a degree in history, as did I, and must have heard from his parents what I was doing with the Park Service. Looking for a possible career change, Jonathan called to chat with me about my work. I had no recollection of him, as we determined we had last met at his fourth birthday party, when I gave him a purple stuffed animal that he claimed to still own. The family moved from Connecticut to Rhode Island, where he spent much of his youth. At the time he called, Jonathan was working at the University of Connecticut, living near Storrs. He said we should get together some time when I came back to visit Connecticut. I must have even mentioned the signers' graves project, at which he expressed an interest in playing along, helping me to find some New England signers' graves.

I returned to Connecticut in February of 2000 to spend some time with my parents. I must have warned Jonathan of my trip north, and we made a plan to meet at my parents' house. Not only did I reunite with a childhood acquaintance, but I was able to add two more signers' graves to the list.

We set out that day to find two Connecticut signers, Oliver Wolcott and Roger Sherman. Wolcott was from Litchfield, only a half hour away from my hometown, and a small town at that. So I was hoping we would not have a lot of trouble locating his grave. Sherman was buried in New Haven, a different story, in that it is a large city with which I was unfamiliar. Compounding the situation was the season—February in Connecticut—and there was snow on the ground.

We began in Litchfield, in what I would call typical New England— the town green, old white church, historic houses. Litchfield has some great history; an early law school attended by Aaron Burr, among others.[81] Litchfield was the birthplace of Harriet Beecher Stowe and the home of one of George Washington's spies, Benjamin Tallmadge.[82] Benjamin Franklin's son William supposedly spent some time in prison in Litchfield.[83] I grew up hearing the story that a statue of King George III

---

81   Peter C. Vermilyea, *Hidden History of Litchfield County* (Charleston, SC: The History Press, 2014), 85.

82   "A Walking Tour of Historic Litchfield," on litchfieldhistoricalsociety.org, accessed on February 3, 2019, https://www.litchfieldhistoricalsociety.org/wp-content/uploads/2018/04/Walking-Tour-Brochure_LHS.pdf.

83   Vermilyea, *Hidden History of Litchfield County*, 27.

from New York City was taken down by angry colonists and melted into bullets for the colonial war effort here in Litchfield. Of most significance to me though, was the East Cemetery and Oliver Wolcott.

I did not realize that Oliver Wolcott and that story about the statue of King George were so intertwined. Thanks to my friend Peter Vermilyea's book on Litchfield County, I learned a fun story that relates to a Declaration signer. Wolcott had returned to Connecticut and missed the vote on independence in the Continental Congress in July 1776. He was returning to Philadelphia and passed through New York City when George Washington had the Declaration read to the troops. Wolcott saw the patriots take down the statue of King George III and offered to send it home to Litchfield to be melted into bullets. He helped with those efforts, counting 42,088 cartridges made from the statue. He returned to Philadelphia and signed the Declaration on October 1, 1776,[84] after most signed in August.

These founding fathers did not make things easy for us later generations, in that they often named their children after themselves. Oliver Wolcott, the signer, had a son, Oliver, Jr., who would go on to play a role in Washington's cabinet as Secretary of the Treasury after Hamilton.[85] This trip was all about finding the grave of Oliver, Sr., the signer. To do so involved tromping through a bit of snow. Being a fairly small cemetery, it did not take us too long to find him, and the snow made for some neat pictures.

As this quest continued, I would come to question whether the signer was actually buried where it said he was buried. Through my work in Washington, DC, I met Becky at the National Archives, who by coincidence

---

84   Vermilyea, *Hidden History of Litchfield County*, 32.

85   Robert G. Ferris, editor, *Signers of the Declaration: Historic Places Commemorating the Signing of the Declaration of Independence* (Washington, DC: United States Department of the Interior, 1975), 152.

Fig 23: Oliver Wolcott's grave, East Cemetery, Litchfield, Connecticut

had worked in Litchfield, and could verify for me that Oliver Wolcott was indeed buried where it said he was buried in Litchfield's East Cemetery.

So then we were off to New Haven—a very different experience than Litchfield. We made the mistake of relying on Mapquest for our directions to the Grove Street Cemetery, right in the midst of the Yale University campus. Maybe it was human error, but we ended up in a very different part of town. The directions we followed had us nowhere near where we wanted to be. That added to the adventure…and frustration. I remember a lot of cursing involved in the name of Mapquest.

When we finally arrived at the Grove Street Cemetery, we were really impressed. What a great old cemetery. Lots of history as one might expect in an old urban New England cemetery. Here lies Eli Whitney, inventor of the cotton gin; David Humphreys, one of Washington's aides; Noah Webster, dictionary writer; and many folks affiliated with Yale.[86] Of course, I was all about finding Roger Sherman. He was pretty significant in the

---

86   "The Grove Street Cemetery," on grovestreetcemetery.org, accessed on February 10, 2019, http://www.grovestreetcemetery.org/.

Connecticut story, having signed all the big founding documents, and having some measure of responsibility for the Connecticut Compromise at the Constitutional Convention. This would help balance the vote in the legislature—Senate would have equal numbers for each state, while the House of Representatives would be based on state population.[87] Sherman's got himself a nice spot and neat markers in this cemetery. There looks to be an old gravestone, and behind it, a more modern marker identifying his grave. It had been snowing when we visited, which made it fun to look at the collection of grave photos in the album. The snow pictures make a nice contrast to all the spring and summer photos. I never really doubted that

Sherman was in the Grove Street Cemetery, and enjoyed the chance to meet up with Jonathan and have him share in the grave hunt.

In preparation for this book, I went online to do some research on New Haven's Grove Street Cemetery. It has a pretty extensive website, with information about tours and plenty of history. I noticed that the cemetery was created in 1797. I checked on information about Roger Sherman, and found that

Fig 24: Roger Sherman's grave, Grove Street Cemetery, New Haven, Connecticut

---

87   John G. Rommel, *Connecticut's Yankee Patriot: Roger Sherman* (Hartford, CT: The American Revolution Bicentennial Commission of Connecticut, 1979), 41.

Sherman died in 1793.[88] That made me wonder—where was Roger Sherman between 1793 and 1797, if that was in fact when he was buried in the new cemetery?

A return trip to New Haven was in order. I happened to have some time to visit in October 2010, and was able to catch a scheduled tour of the cemetery. I was anxious to have a chance to ask about Roger Sherman's original burial place, as I am sure he must have rested some place upon his death.

As a group began to form at the cemetery entrance for the morning tour, my dad jumped right in and told the guide we were on a specific mission. When I asked where Sherman was originally buried, she told me that most people were buried on the New Haven Green before the Grove Street Cemetery opened. I followed up with a question about when he was moved. Here is where it got confusing. At one point during the tour, she said everyone was moved from the New Haven Green. At another point on the tour, it sounded like she said many bodies were left behind on the Green and never moved. At the end of the tour, I tried to get clarification, and she suggested I speak with Bill at the caretaker's building at the entrance. Bill had been working at the Grove Street Cemetery for many many years with hardly a day off.

I asked him about the date of the newer Sherman stone, and he sent me over to it, saying he knew the date was on it but he couldn't remember with all the different dates associated with this cemetery. The back of the newer stone said 1941. The tour guide claimed the older stone was moved from the New Haven Green. It looked almost like a table, with a stone lying horizontally on top of five short legs, supposedly one for each of the documents Sherman signed, and the fifth for his term as governor.

---

88   "The Grove Street Cemetery," on grovestreetcemetery.org, accessed on February 10, 2019, http://www.grovestreetcemetery.org/.

When I returned from my search for the date, I asked Bill when Sherman was moved. He shook his head and said there are no records to indicate Sherman was ever moved. He concluded, "He's not here."

Wow! Another grave shocker. For years I had thought Sherman was peacefully resting at the Grove Street Cemetery. Now it appears his remains lie unmarked with many other unknowns on the New Haven Green. This required a trip to the Green. After a brief stop for pizza my dad and I were off to the Green, a large open space in the middle of New Haven. Three churches are on the Green, including one with a few grave-stones behind it. I enjoyed my walk around the Green, which included a conversation with a local who told me all about Yale owning the city. While I am still unclear as to Sherman's final resting place, this further adds to the collection of Declaration signers who have been moved or are missing. I thought this one was a sure thing, with the stone in the cemetery, but by asking a few questions, it appears there is a whole dif-ferent story. That is what makes this project so fascinating.

Fig 25 and 26: Plaque on church, and Center Church on the Green, New Haven, Connecticut

IX

New Jersey

2 000 was a big year for the grave hunt. I visited a lot of sites that year, as my obsession with this project really took hold. I pored over my favorite website, findagrave.com, and plotted out trips to see how many graves I could hit in a day or a weekend. In my vocabulary, it even became a verb—graving, to go in search of signers' graves. As a kid who never liked to stray from home, boy had I changed. I loved being on the road and exploring new places, which sometimes meant being out late driving. This worried my parents, who hated my being out on the road, before the days when everyone carried a cell phone. The easiest solution was not to worry them by not telling them.

This was the case one spring day when I decided to make some signer stops on my way to a family gathering in suburban New York City. I chose to take the scenic route through Trenton, and Princeton, New Jersey. On my agenda was finding the graves of George Clymer in Trenton and John Witherspoon and Richard Stockton in Princeton.

What a contrast in destinations. Princeton is a quaint, historic university town, while Trenton, no offense to Trentonians, is a very urban area, at least the part I saw. It was one of those times that it was better off that my parents didn't know where I was by myself, even in the middle of the day. Luckily I found the Friends Meeting House fairly easily. It is a pretty small building, quietly sitting on a corner in the midst of Trenton. Having grown up in a very small town, this was probably not my favorite spot, especially on my own. I was slightly nervous walking away from my car, even for a short distance, but it was all in the name of history and finding another grave. Not only was this the time before everyone had a cell phone, but it was also before a GPS was in every car, so finding these places was a little trickier than it might be today.

Upon arriving on site, I encountered the most frustrating element of this crusade—the locked gate. The meeting house sits on a corner, and maybe because of the neighborhood, an iron gate keeps access to the yard impossible. I walked around all sides and thought I saw a little flag under a tree. The placement of the building and the fence made it difficult to confirm if that was indeed Clymer's grave. The zoom lens didn't quite make it, and there was no getting into the yard. How frustrating.

Fig 27: George Clymer's grave marked by flag under tree, Friends Meeting House, Trenton, New Jersey

I remember thinking though, that the fence wasn't that tall. Not being agile myself, I knew I couldn't climb over it, but maybe one of my friends could. So I checked Clymer off the list, but marked it with a star, as a site I would like to return to someday with back up.

Next it was on to Princeton. If I'd been there before, I didn't remember it. What a neat town. I stopped off at the Princeton Battlefield, commemorating the January 1777 battle. This was another victory for General Washington after his successful surprise attack on the Hessian soldiers in Trenton on Christmas 1776, after crossing the Delaware River. I hiked around the battlefield, then drove through downtown by the Princeton University campus and on to Princeton Cemetery, a great old cemetery. Many famous people are buried there, including President Grover Cleveland and politician Aaron Burr, famous for the fatal duel with Alexander Hamilton. While I took photos of those graves too, I was more concerned with a Declaration signer. This time it was John Witherspoon, a president of Princeton University, and also the only clergyman to sign the Declaration of Independence. Witherspoon was originally from Scotland and came to the colonies to serve as president of the school, then known as the College of New Jersey. Many of the early university presidents are buried together in one section of this old cemetery.[89] Unlike some I've visited, the Princeton Cemetery was well-kept, reflecting a community concerned with its history.

This interest in preservation must not have always been the case. An article from the *Continental Monthly*, from January 1862, refers to a notice posted near the Presidents' Plot to discourage vandalism, written by a college professor, Dr. Giger:

---

89   "Brochure and Map," on Princeton Cemetery of Nassau Presbyterian Church, accessed on February 10, 2019, http://nassauchurch.org/wp-content/uploads/2016/05/PrCemGuide2016WebVersion.pdf.

KEEP YOUR SACRILEGIOUS HANDS OFF THESE VENERABLE STONES! PARIAN MARBLE, WROUGHT WITH CONSUMMATE SKILL, COULD NOT REPLACE THEM. CONNECTED WITH THESE HOMELY MONUMENTS ARE HISTORICAL ASSOCIATIONS THAT OUGHT NOT TO BE FORGOTTEN. THE SCARCITY OF BETTER MATERIALS, THE RUDENESS OF MONUMENTAL SCULPTURE, THE POVERTY OF THE COUNTRY, THE EARLY STRUGGLES AND PECUNIARY EMBARRASSMENTS OF THE COLONY, AT THE PERIOD WHEN THESE MONUMENTS WERE ERECTED, AS WELL AS THE SELF-DENIAL AND HARDSHIPS AND LABORS OF THE DISTINGUISHED MEN WHO GAVE FAME AND USEFULNESS TO NASSAU HALL, ARE INDICATED BY THESE ROUGH STONES. NOTHING MODERN, NOTHING POLISHED OR MAGNIFICENT, COULD SUGGEST THE EARLY HISTORY OF NEW JERSEY. SPARE WHAT REMAINS OF THESE BROKEN MEMORIALS. THOUGHTLESS YOUNG MAN! WHY DO YOU BREAK AND DEFACE THESE OLD MONUMENTS? A FEW FRAGMENTS CARRIED IN YOUR POCKET, OR PLACED IN YOUR CABINET, WILL NOT IMPART TO YOU THE ACTIVITY AND ENERGY OF BURR, OR THE PROFOUND AND LOGICAL INTELLECT OF EDWARDS, OR THE ELOQUENCE OF DAVIES, OR THE PIETY AND TRIUMPHANT DEATH OF FINLEY, OR THE POETICAL WISDOM, THE POWER OF GOVERNING AND INSPIRING YOUTH, THE LOVE OF KNOWLEDGE, AND THE STERN UNFLINCHING PATRIOTISM OF WITHERSPOON. IF YOU ADMIRE AND REVERENCE THE CHARACTER OF THESE GREAT AND GOOD MEN, READ THEIR WORKS, AND IMITATE THEIR EXAMPLE; AND FORBEAR, WE BESEECH YOU, TO ADD

TO THE SHAMEFUL MUTILATION OF THE FRAIL MEMORIALS
INTENDED TO PROTECT THEIR BONES FROM INSULT.[90]

Upon finding this passage, I knew I had to include it here. Obviously this is specific to the Princeton Cemetery, as it refers to numerous presidents of today's Princeton University, but the sentiment can certainly be expanded to include many of the cemeteries I visited during this adventure. It is fascinating that this was in a journal in 1862. This really embodies the motivation for my grave hunt, as I was so surprised by the lack of respect in death for these American patriots. Princeton's situation was not unique; remember Jefferson's grave being chipped away at soon after his burial as one example. The journal cited claimed this was placed in the Presidents' Plot, "to prevent, if possible, further mutilation, the following unique and elaborate, but eloquent notice, enclosed in an iron frame, had been placed over the graves of these reverend fathers."[91] I don't recall seeing such a sign upon visiting the cemetery recently, but wanted to incorporate the message into the story.

The question I have come to ask at each signer's grave now is whether or not the man is really buried in the grave. I have no reason to doubt that Rev. John Witherspoon is not buried in the Princeton Cemetery. He died at the age of 72 in 1794, still serving as college president, and nearly blind.[92] He lived in Princeton, and there are accounts of his funeral. The Princeton Cemetery had already established the plot for

---

90 "The Graveyard at Princeton," *The Continental Monthly*, January 1862, Vol 1, Issue 1, 32.

91 "The Graveyard at Princeton," *The Continental Monthly*, January 1862, Vol 1, Issue 1, 32.

92 B.J. Lossing, *Lives of the Signers of the Declaration of Independence* (1848; repr., Aledo, TX: WallBuilder Press, 1998), 84.

the college presidents by 1794, so it seems to indicate Witherspoon remains where he was originally laid to rest.

My day of graving was not done yet. I remember proclaiming, on a day such as this when I had essentially found three graves, that it was a banner day for graving. My last stop was just off the Princeton Battlefield at the Stony Brook Quaker Meeting House Burial Ground. This was the place for prominent Princeton folks to be buried before the establishment of the Princeton Cemetery in 1757.[93] Here I was looking for Richard Stockton.

Fig 28: Rev. John Witherspoon's grave, Princeton Cemetery, Princeton, New Jersey

Richard Stockton came from a long line of Stocktons in this area. Today one can keep track of the family by visiting their home, Morven, to learn of the many generations of the Stockton family and their long influence on American history. One of the sadder Declaration signer stories, Stockton was imprisoned on a ship in New York Harbor by the British during the Revolution and forever suffered the consequences, dying a broken man in 1781 at the age of 50.[94] For signers who lived in areas where the war was fought, life was often more difficult. Attaching their name to the Declaration of Independence was not a simple decision, and was not ignored by the British, especially early in the war when the outcome

---

93 "Brochure and Map," on Princeton Cemetery of Nassau Presbyterian Church, accessed on February 10, 2019, http://nassauchurch.org/wp-content/uploads/2016/05/PrCemGuide2016WebVersion.pdf.

94 Ferris, *Signers of the Declaration: Historic Places Commemorating the Signing of the Declaration of Independence*, 134-135.

was still unknown. With the British army entrenched in the Philadelphia vicinity, those signers from the middle colonies really suffered.

I found the Quaker Meeting House pretty easily. A small house stands next to a fenced-in yard. I made my way into the yard, and fairly quickly found the stone I was looking for, the marker for Richard Stockton. However, I was not so pleased with the message on the stone: "Richard Stockton, a signer of the Declaration of Independence is buried in these grounds, 1730-1781." My immediate thought, with no one else around, a thought I probably verbalized while standing there, was how is it possible that this well respected signer of the Declaration could be buried in this yard, and no one know for sure where? I would pose this question many times. I remember hearing at Berkeley Plantation how there was a fear of the British possibly trying to do something awful to the bodies of patriots if the war had ended differently. In that case, maybe graves were deliberately left unmarked. With all the suffering that Richard Stockton had gone through, this might have been a possibility. On a visit to Morven, I asked if anyone knew anything more about Richard Stockton's grave and got nothing further.

Thankfully, the Princeton Library has compiled a wonderful online resource with many links to historic references. One source is the 1879 *History of Princeton and Its Institutions*, a two-volume set by John Frelinghuysen Hageman. This work provides insight into the Stockton grave situation with this explanation:

RICHARD STOCKTON, THE SIGNER OF THE DECLARATION,
WAS BURIED THERE, AND THERE IS NO MONUMENT TO
MARK HIS GRAVE. IT IS A PECULIARITY OF THE QUAKERS
WHICH FORBIDS THE USE OF TOMBSTONES OR MONUMENTS
OF ANY KIND TO DESIGNATE ONE GRAVE FROM ANOTHER,
OR PERPETUATE THE NAMES OF THE DEAD. THIS CUSTOM
IS ATTENDED WITH A GREAT DISADVANTAGE TO THE
HISTORIAN WHO IS SEARCHING FOR FAMILY GENEALOGIES
AND THE DATES OF IMPORTANT DEATHS.[95]

This custom also affects those in search of all the graves of Declaration signers. While it is disappointing not to know the exact burial location, this reason makes sense. It seems likely that Stockton's remains were placed in this yard and left unmarked for religious reasons. The plaque was added in 1913 by the New Jersey Society of the Sons of the American Revolution.

Fig 29 and 30: Richard Stockton's stone, Stony Brook Quaker
Meeting House, Princeton, New Jersey

95   John Frelinghuysen Hageman, *History of Princeton and Its Institutions, Vol. II* (Philadelphia, PA: J.B. Lippincott & Co., 1879), 415.

By the time I made it to dinner that night with the family in New York, I had plenty of stories to share about my findings—the frustrations of the locked gate in Trenton, the exact location unknown in Princeton—but overall, a sense of accomplishment that I could check off three more graves from the list. Well, almost—one was marked with an asterisk to hopefully return at a later date for further investigation.

X

Close to Home: Part Two

Some days this grave hunt provided a real challenge. Other days proved rather effortless, especially when an organization like the National Park Service sets aside a national historic site in honor of a Declaration signer. This was the case in looking for the grave of Maryland signer, Thomas Stone. Stone's property, located in Port Tobacco, Maryland, about an hour outside Washington, DC, remained in the family for six generations. It opened as a historic site in 1997.[96]

I made the trip to Port Tobacco on a day off in April of 2000. I am pretty sure I had the place to myself. Not the busiest of national parks, the site has made some major improvements since my first visit, including a visitor center. I took the tour through the house and tried to learn all I could about Thomas Stone, a signer I knew very little about before this

---

96 "Frequently Asked Questions, Thomas Stone National Historic Site," on https://www. nps.gov/thst/faqs.htm, accessed on February 23, 2019, https://www.nps.gov/thst/faqs. htm.

visit. Maybe that is why his biography is titled *Thomas Stone: Elusive Maryland Signer*. Early in the book, Stone is described as:

> RUGGED, RETICENT AND RESERVED. THOMAS STONE IS ONE OF THE LEAST CONSPICUOUS OF MARYLAND'S GREAT REVOLUTIONARY HEROES NOT BECAUSE HE WAS NOT ENTITLED TO THE PLAUDITS OF THE ENTHUSIASTS OF THE REPUBLIC THEN IN THE MAKING, BUT BECAUSE HE SHUNNED NOTORIETY, AND IT WAS ONLY GIVEN TO A FEW INTIMATE ASSOCIATES TO KNOW THE TRUE WORTH OF THE MAN.[97]

My main focus, of course, was the family graveyard not too far from the house. On that first trip I took the grave at face value, probably using an entire roll of film (yes, film) to document the grave for the collection. I remember on a subsequent visit, after discovering some of the quirky situations with other signer graves, asking Ranger Scott how confident he was that Thomas Stone was buried in the yard on the property. Ranger Scott believes that Stone is buried in the family yard and then relayed to me the sad story of Stone's death. In 1787, Stone was elected to serve in the Constitutional Convention, but declined because his wife was ill. When she died he was so distraught he decided to take a trip to England. He was to leave from Alexandria, Virginia, and while waiting for a ship to take him across the ocean, he died. Some authors have speculated that he died of a broken heart.

Ranger Scott shared this letter that Thomas Stone sent to his son on October 1, 1787.

---

97   John M. and Roberta J. Wearmouth, *Thomas Stone: Elusive Maryland Signer* (Port Tobacco, MD: Stones Throw Publishing, 1984), 15.

My Dear Frederick:

I am now in a weak state, about to travel, and probably shall not see you more. Let me intreat you to attend to the following advice, which I leave you as a legacy; keep and read it, and resort to it. In the first place, do your duty to God in spirit and in truth, always considering Him as your best protector, and doing all things to please Him...Think more

Fig 31: Thomas Stone's grave, Port Tobacco, Maryland

of your soul's health and the next world than of this, and never do wrong on any account...Seek the company of sober, virtuous and good people... Seek to do all the good you can, remembering that there is no happiness equal to that which good actions accord...Take care not to be seduced by the professions of any person to do what your heart tells you is wrong, for on self-approbation all happiness depends...Let your aim in life be to attain the goodness rather than greatness among men: The former is solid, the latter all vanity, and often leads to ruin...This I speak from experience...I commend you to Heaven's protection. May God of His infinite mercy protect you and lead you to happiness in this world and the next is the most

FERVENT PRAYER OF YOUR LOVING FATHER.[98]

Stone died on October 5, 1787.[99]

Fig 32: Stone family cemetery, Port Tobacco, Maryland

---

98   Wearmouth, *Thomas Stone: Elusive Signer*, 116–117.

99   Lossing, *Lives of the Signers*, 153.

XI

New York City

Growing up in Connecticut, I had many opportunities to visit New York City. Usually it was for the holiday decorations in the store windows or the tree at Rockefeller Center. Knowing there was plenty of history to see there, my friend and co-worker Michael and I planned a weekend trip to visit some historic sites in 2000. We wandered around Manhattan, visiting Federal Hall, the site of George Washington's first inauguration located on Wall Street, just down the block from Trinity Church. Many historic figures are buried in the Trinity Churchyard—Alexander Hamilton, first Secretary of the Treasury and famous victim of the duel with Aaron Burr; Albert Gallatin, Jefferson's Secretary of the Treasury; and of importance to the grave hunt, Francis Lewis, New York signer of the Declaration of Independence.[100]

---

100 "Famous Memorials in Trinity Churchyard," on findagrave.com, accessed on February 19, 2019, https://www.findagrave.com/cemetery/230947/famous-memorials?page=1#sr-8369419.

Not one of the more famous Declaration signers, Francis Lewis was born in Wales and orphaned as a young child. He came to the colonies and amassed a fortune as a merchant, which he would lose during the Revolution.[101] Sadly, he suffered an even greater loss when his wife was captured by the British during the war and he never fully recovered, dying in 1779. Lewis' property, which was destroyed by the British, stood approximately where the Whitestone Bridge is today in Queens, New York.[102] A local park honors Francis Lewis right under the bridge.[103]

Sources vary on Francis Lewis' death date; most indicate December 1802. According to the Trinity Church website, Lewis was buried on January 1, 1803, which may lead to the confusion—when the date of death and date of burial happen in different years. Most sources indicate that Lewis was buried in an unmarked grave. A plaque was placed in the churchyard in 1947. It reads: "Near this spot are interred the remains of/ Francis Lewis, 1713-1803/Signer of the Declaration of Independence/ Vestryman of Trinity Church/Erected by the Society of/the Descendants of the Signers/of the Declaration of Independence/1947."[104] In New Jersey I learned that it was a Quaker tradition not to mark graves at the time of burial. I have not found anything that specifies why Lewis' grave was not marked. Alexander Hamilton, who died around the same time, had his grave marked. So another mystery exists when it comes to the exact location of the remains of Francis Lewis. It is yet another sad

---

101 Paul J. Scudiere, *New York's Signers of the Declaration of Independence* (Albany, NY: New York State American Revolution Bicentennial Commission, 1975), 25.

102 Scudiere, *New York's Signers of the Declaration of Independence*, 27-28.

103 "Francis Lewis Park," on nycgovparks.org, accessed on February 19, 2019, https:// www.nycgovparks.org/parks/francis-lewis-park/history.

104 "Lewis, Francis" on registers.trinitywallstreet.org, accessed on February 19, 2019, https://registers.trinitywallstreet.org/files/history/churchyard/history.php?area_ id=4&id=440#here.

ending for a signer who suffered great consequences for the brave act of signing the Declaration of Independence.

Fig 33: Francis Lewis' stone, Trinity Churchyard, New York, New York

We were very lucky to have fabulous accommodations with my cousins Debbie and John, who graciously hosted us in their New York City apartment on more than one occasion. Michael and I returned to Manhattan in January 2001 to tour some sites, including the Statue of Liberty and Ellis Island. We have some great pictures from that trip standing on Liberty Island, looking out at the Twin Towers. Also on the agenda for that weekend was a trip to the Bronx, in search of the grave of Lewis Morris. In his day, Morris owned a lot of property and a large home known as Morrisania.[105] Today, this urban area of the Bronx would be a real contrast to Morris' sprawling estate. I remember poring over the map of the Bronx, plotting out where we would get off the subway in order to easily find the church where Morris was buried. I am lucky to have

105 Scudiere, *New York's Signers of the Declaration of Independence*, 13.

friends who would make this trip with me, and relatives who would let me stay with them while on this quest. Of all the graves I would search for, Lewis Morris' would prove the greatest challenge.

Finding St. Ann's Church was not too difficult. But again we would encounter the frustrating locked gate. It was winter time, with snow on the ground. A sign on the lawn of the church identified this as the burial place of Lewis Morris. As we stood on the sidewalk, looking longingly toward the church grounds locked to us, a man walking his dog came by.

He stopped to talk to us, probably wondering why we would be standing outside this locked gate on a cold day in the Bronx. As it turned out, he worked at the church as a caretaker, and after hearing why we were there he offered to let us in. I could not believe our good luck. He opened the gate and showed us the tomb on the hill, visible from the sidewalk. He thought this was the grave we were looking for, but it was the grave of Morris' half-brother Gouvernor, a prominent member of the Constitutional Convention. Our guide must have thought I asked about this Morris brother. Gouvernor's tomb has another gate on it, because one can go down into where the body rests. The man offered us the opportunity to do this, which we certainly could not turn down. Then he gave us a quick tour inside the church. I'll never forget walking down the aisle in the church and seeing the grave of Gouvernor Morris' mother under my feet. When a more recent church building was constructed, it was built right over Mrs. Morris' grave. All of this was fascinating, however it did not serve to accomplish the mission.

It was hard to ask for more after seeing all of this cool history, but one big question remained—where was Lewis Morris buried? I finally asked our host if he knew where Lewis was buried. Yes, he knew. He was in the church basement. Now we were getting somewhere. We walked around toward the back of the building, to see the cellar door—locked.

Our guide said he had a key, but since he was out walking the dog and not working, he did not have the key with him. But he assured us that if we made arrangements to come back, we would have no problem getting into the basement to see Lewis Morris' grave. He told us to contact the church the next time we are in town, and we could make it happen. Excited by the history we saw, but disappointed in not completing the mission, we left the Bronx that day, optimistic in our chances of getting at this grave another time. If only it would be that easy.

Fig 34: Gouvernor Morris' tomb, St. Ann's Church,
The Bronx, New York

Fig 35: St. Ann's Church lawn, The
Bronx, New York

XII

York, PA and Delaware

When I began working at the National Mall I quickly made friends with Ernie, mostly because of a common interest in baseball. I was a huge fan of the sport while in high school, rooting with my family for the New York Mets in 1986. After going off to college in Pennsylvania, I halfheartedly followed the Phillies and the nearby Orioles. Ernie is a big Orioles fan and that first summer at the National Mall he introduced me to the world of minor league baseball. We easily could go catch a game after work to see the Bowie Baysox or Frederick Keys. What fun it is now to recognize players we watched in the minors make it to the big leagues; we watched Jayson Werth catch for Baltimore in the minors. What does this have to do with the search for the signers? During the summer of 2000, while seriously enthralled with the grave hunt, I also tried to include trips to minor league ballparks in my travels. Why not coordinate both hobbies? Clearly the obsessive collector trait gene kicked in, as that summer was all about the grave photos and the souvenir plastic stadium soda cups—quite the combination.

On another of my weekdays off, in early August of 2000, I decided to head north to find the two graves in York, Pennsylvania, and maybe if time, make it all the way to New Castle, Delaware, to find the George Read grave. After consulting my main source, findagrave.com, I was off. The first stop was to find James Smith in downtown York at the First Presbyterian Church. Not one of the more famous signers, especially when considering the more prominent men among the Pennsylvania delegation, Smith was born in Ireland and came to America during his childhood. He spent a long time as a lawyer, living until 1806, but before his death his house burned down, destroying a lot of his papers. Many sources assume that is why so little is known about Smith, though his work demonstrates his patriot leanings. He raised a militia company in York and spoke favorably about independence. Smith was elected to the Continental Congress in late July 1776, but arrived in time to sign his name on the Declaration.[106]

According to the website of the First Presbyterian Church, the current building dates to the Civil War era. The original church building, dating to just after the Revolution, was located on the same land. The website claims the cemetery outside the building has 175 people buried in it, "representing many well-known families from the 18th and 19th centuries."[107]

Usually, the sign that someone wasn't originally buried in his current plot comes from the dates. Here they seem to work out, in that Smith, who because of his militia unit received the honorary title of colonel, died in 1806, while the original church building was completed in 1793.

---

106   Ferris, *Signers of the Declaration: Historic Places Commemorating the Signing of the Declaration of Independence*, 132-133.

107   "Our History," on First Presbyterian Church of York, accessed on February 19, 2019, http://www.fpcyork.org/about-us/history/.

I have not come across anything that would lead me to believe that Smith isn't really there or was moved from another location. He died in York, although that doesn't necessarily guarantee anything, as we shall see in the next York grave visit. The commonwealth did put up a historical marker, but as seen in the James Wilson chapter, markers can sometimes mislead too.

Fig 36: James Smith's grave, First Presbyterian Church, York, Pennsylvania

Before finishing the James Smith story, I just have to mention that when I look back over the collection of grave photos and contemplate all the travels, I have to call this my favorite photograph. The folks in York do a great job with the flowers and I happened to catch this one on a beautiful day. But this was just the first stop on a busy day. Next it was off to find Philip Livingston.

The Livingstons were a prominent New York family. Many members were involved in business and politics. Philip's cousin Robert served on the committee that drafted the Declaration of Independence, yet ironically, never signed the document. He was back in New York when the signing took place. Robert went on to participate in other historical moments, serving as the Chancellor of New York, who was responsible for administering the oath of office to President George Washington. He also was involved in the negotiation of the Louisiana Purchase.[108] Philip's career would not have the same longevity as his cousin Robert's.

---

108 Lossing, *Lives of the Signers of the Declaration of Independence*, 241.

Philip was reelected to the Continental Congress in 1777. With threats from the British in Philadelphia, the Congress moved its operations to York, Pennsylvania, from September 1777 to June of 1778. Philip Livingston felt obligated to attend, although his health was deteriorating. Supposedly when he left his home in New York, Philip said goodbye to all his family members, as if he knew he would not return home. He died while in York serving in the Congress in June 1778 at the age of 62. A son serving with General Washington rushed to his father's side to be with Philip when he died. Philip Livingston originally was buried in the

churchyard of the German Reformed Church on West Market Street.[109] Apparently the church needed room to expand, so graves there were moved across town to the Prospect Hill Cemetery, which was founded in 1849 and had its first burials two years later. A *York Daily Record* article cited a 1907 *History of York, PA, Volume 1,* by George Prowell with the date Livingston's remains were moved—January 1856.[110]

Fig 37: Philip Livingston's grave, Prospect Hill Cemetery, York, Pennsylvania

If the Prospect Hill Cemetery didn't begin burials until 1851, and

---

109 Jim McClure, "Statesman Philip Livingston buried in York: 'He said his farewells to his family…'" *York Daily Record.* October 12, 2007. Accessed February 20, 2019. https://www.ydr.com/story/news/history/blogs/york-town-square/2007/10/12/post-141/31554821/.

110 Stephen H. Smith, "Declaration signer Philip Livingston monuments in York before the Woolworth's marker." *York Daily Record.* December 7, 2018. Accessed February 20, 2019. https://www.ydr.com/story/news/history/blogs/yorkspast/2018/12/07/livingston-monuments-in-york-before-the-woolworths-marker/38688561/.

Livingston died in 1778, then this is similar to the Roger Sherman situation. Sherman died before the Grove Street Cemetery opened, was buried on the New Haven Green, and when others were moved to the new cemetery, he apparently was left behind. With all that time passing, how can anyone be sure that Livingston's remains made it to the second cemetery? There is another interesting element to this story. In the early 1900s, the expanded church was torn down and eventually replaced by a Woolworth's store. A plaque was placed at the store to mark Livingston's original burial site. When the store closed in 1997, the plaque was moved to the Zion United Church of Christ, where supposedly it can still be seen today.[111]

Here is another signer moved from his original burial place. The circumstances may all be different, but it is so interesting that so many of these men met similar fates.

This day of graving was not over yet. Since I found these two rather quickly, I decided to try for one more: George Read in New Castle, Delaware. At this point, keeping in mind my interest in catching ball games, I also wanted to try to see the Wilmington Blue Rocks play that evening. So the mission continued.

George Read, for those that enjoy the musical 1776, is the Delaware delegate who is against independence and always votes with those from the Deep South. He is portrayed as arguing with his fellow delegates, patriots Rodney and McKean; at least part of that portrayal is accurate. Read was the only one to vote against independence on July 2, and decided to sign the Declaration when it was approved by the Continental Congress. He continued on with a political career that included

---

111   Stephen H. Smith, "Declaration signer Philip Livingston monuments in York before the Woolworth's marker." *York Daily Record*. December 7, 2018. Accessed February 20, 2019. https://www.ydr.com/story/news/history/blogs/yorkspast/2018/12/07/livingston-monuments-in-york-before-the-woolworths-marker/38688561/.

signing the Constitution. Read was buried in the churchyard of the Immanuel Episcopal Church in New Castle, Delaware.[112] Visiting New Castle was a flashback for me, as I think we stopped there for lunch on the trip I took to Washington, DC, with my grandparents. My childhood memories are not the strongest, but I don't think I enjoyed that lunch in New Castle. When I returned looking for the grave of George Read I had a better time. Since I had already been to York, it was late in the day. A return to New Castle to explore the Green is still on the to-do list, but it seemed from my brief stay to be a quaint historic town worthy of further exploration.

The Immanuel Church building suffered a fire and was rebuilt in the 1980s. The website claims that graves in the cemetery date back to 1707. Read died in 1798 and seemed to have been a fairly active member in the church community.[113] I have not come across anything that makes me suspect Read had been moved, but in this story anything is possible.

This weekend proved to be very successful. A three-grave day was especially productive. But I still had one more thing to check off my list. I continued on to Wilmington, hoping to catch the Blue Rocks and

Fig 38: George Read's grave, Immanuel Churchyard, New Castle, Delaware

---

112 Ferris, *Signers of the Declaration: Historic Places Commemorating the Signing of the Declaration of Independence*, 118-119.

113 "History of Immanuel," on immanuelonthegreen.org, accessed February 20, 2019, https://www.immanuelonthegreen.org/History/history-of-immanuel.html.

add to my souvenir baseball park plastic cup collection. It was a weekday, but the crowd still seemed pretty quiet when I pulled into the stadium. I happened to see a couple of buses loading up as I pulled in. The people getting on the buses appeared to be ball players. I couldn't believe my bad luck—the Wilmington Blue Rocks had just finished playing a day game and I had arrived just in time to see both teams boarding the buses to head out. So as I made the long ride home to DC that evening, I had to keep reminding myself about the three graves I found, and not focus on my inability to read a baseball schedule properly.

XIII

Philadelphia

A three-grave day…that was going to be hard to beat. But when my next weekend rolled around, I was up for the challenge.

I have always loved historic Philadelphia. There is something so special about Independence Hall, standing in the room where the United States government was formed. Imagine the conversations that happened within those walls over the years. That is probably why the musical *1776* struck such a chord with me. Besides the snappy show tunes, it portrayed the delegates of the Continental Congress as human beings with all of their eccentricities. History came alive and was more than the boring dates and acts that school students complain about and never remember. I was so excited to visit Independence Hall and the Liberty Bell on my first visit with my family and have loved going back each time.

Once, soon after moving to Washington, DC, for my job at the National Mall, I went to Philadelphia with a bunch of co-workers. We wandered around the historic area and walked by the Christ Church Burial Ground. We were confronted by the always popular locked gate. This was probably 1999 or early 2000, when I was just beginning to get crazy about this project. I remember being disappointed, but not crushed that we couldn't get into this cemetery. I don't think this consumed me as much as it would later; I was just out with some friends visiting Philadelphia, not so focused on the grave hunt. I figured with so many friends I knew who had worked at Independence National Historical Park, someone would help me on a return trip. This would be quite a find too—there were five signers in this one burial ground.

I was probably calmer about the whole thing, in that I felt like they threw us a bone, because one grave at least was partially accessible.

The most famous person in the Christ Church Burial Ground is arguably Benjamin Franklin. He designed his own simple headstone and left in his will how it should be marked:

"I wish to be buried by the side of my wife, if it may be, and that a marble stone to be made by Chambers, six feet long, four feet wide, plain, with only a small moulding round the upper edge, and this inscription

Benjamin
and Franklin
Deborah[114]

---

114   Sherman Day, *Historical Collections of the State of Pennsylvania* (Philadelphia: George W. Gorton, 1843). 576.

Fig 39: Benjamin Franklin's grave, Christ Church Burial Ground, Philadelphia, Pennsylvania

When one visits today, one also finds a plaque nearby with the epitaph a young Franklin wrote in 1728:

THE BODY OF

B. FRANKLIN, PRINTER,

LIKE THE COVER OF AN OLD BOOK,

ITS CONTENTS TORN OUT,

AND STRIPT OF ITS LETTERING & GILDING

LIES HERE. FOOD FOR WORMS.

BUT THE WORK SHALL NOT BE LOST.

FOR IT WILL AS HE BELIEV'D,

APPEAR ONCE MORE

IN A NEW AND MORE ELEGANT EDITION

CORRECTED AND IMPROVED
BY THE AUTHOR. [115]

Fig 40: Marker at Franklin's grave, Christ Church Burial Ground, Philadelphia, Pennsylvania

His funeral in 1790 attracted a huge crowd. He was buried on the edge of the burial ground at 5th and Arch streets. So when one goes to visit and the cemetery gate is locked, a visitor can still pay his respects to Ben Franklin. His descendants were extremely considerate of those of us interested in graves, for in 1858 they requested iron bars be inserted in front of Franklin's grave.[116] A recent article disagrees with the family story. Boston, the city of Franklin's birth, seemed annoyed that Philadelphia had forgotten Franklin. Boston built a statue to honor Franklin and had a fancy unveiling party for his 150th birthday in 1856. Not to be outdone, Philadelphia realized it had the real thing—Ben himself, and maybe the city had not done enough to remember its hero.

---

115 "Benjamin Franklin…In His Own Words," on www.loc.gov/exhibits/franklin/franklin-epitaph.html, accessed on February 23, 2019, www.loc.gov/exhibits/franklin/franklin-epitaph.html.

116 Jean K. Wolf, *Lives of the Silent Stones in the Christ Church Burial Ground: 50 Family Profiles* (Philadelphia, PA: Christ Church Preservation Trust, 2003), 10.

WITH HOW MUCH...PROPRIETY MAY THE AMERICAN BLUSH WITH SELF-CONDEMNATION AT THE THOUGHT OF ALLOWING 68 YEARS TO ROLL OVER THE TOMB OF ONE OF OUR COUNTRYMEN WHO, EVEN WHILE LIVING, WROTE HIS EPITAPH ON THE CLOUDS OF HEAVEN WITH A PEN OF LIGHTNING, AND YET WHOSE GRAVE IS NOT MARKED WITH A TRIBUTARY MONUMENT?[117]

While some of Philadelphia's leading citizens who were affiliated with the Franklin Institute were behind the wall project, they made it look like it was being done for the people, to build interest in the project and capitalize on Franklin's memory. They claimed it was "to relieve the tombstone of the illustrious philosopher and patriot from the concealment which has not ceased to obscure it for nearly 70 years."[118] This seems like an elaborate rouse to make Franklin's grave accessible to the public. Nowadays, one will often find pennies tossed on Franklin's grave, as it was said to bring good luck, even if Franklin insisted that "a penny saved is a penny earned." The burial ground has undergone a restoration project recently due to the damage the pennies have caused to Franklin's stone.[119]

Franklin may be the most well-known, but he is not the only Declaration signer resting at the Christ Church Burial Ground. After that visit with my friends, I was already thinking about how to get into that locked gate to find the rest of the signers' graves. I was not too worried though,

---

117   Mark Dixon, "How Franklin's Grave Became a Monument and Philadelphians Were Persuaded to Like It," *Hidden City Philadelphia*, April 19, 2017, accessed on March 16, 2019. https://hiddencityphila.org/2017/04/behind-the-publicity-stunt-at-benjamin-franklins-grave/.

118   Dixon, "How Franklin's Grave Became a Monument and Philadelphians Were Persuaded to Like It."

119   "Benjamin Franklin's grave pitted from pennies needs makeover," *The Seattle Times*, November 14, 2016, accessed on February 23, 2019, https://www.seattletimes.com/nation-world/benjamin-franklins-gravestone-develops-crack-from-pennies/.

because over the years I knew I would be back to visit Independence National Historical Park, which includes the Liberty Bell, Independence Hall, and a bit of the historic area around these sites. It turned out to be easier than I thought. Park rangers at Independence did walking tours at the Christ Church Burial Ground occasionally, so I was able to get in that way. They did not do them very often, but luckily one tour coincided with my mid-week days off.

As I've said, I was very lucky to have friends with similar interests and days off willing to trek with me to historic sites or graves. I met Jerry on my first day at work at the National Mall; we started the same day as permanent park employees, although he had worked there the summer before so he could show me the ropes. He had also worked at Independence Hall and was particularly interested in the Declaration story. He shares an interest in 1776 and has attended a movie-viewing party at my house. As relatively new employees, we both enjoyed our mid-week days off, so Jerry was willing to come along on several grave-hunting adventures. His knowledge and contacts at Independence could prove useful too.

We had a very ambitious schedule ahead of us for this day trip to Philadelphia. Not only were there the five signers, counting Franklin, at the Christ Church Burial Ground, but two more signers buried just outside Christ Church. The burial ground is about four blocks from the church. As I would learn later, churches often did not get land right near the building for their cemeteries, so they could be blocks away. A sign outside the burial ground explains that there was no room for burials near the church and that land nearby was too marshy. We even had hopes of hitting one more grave on the way home, that of John Morton the first of the signers to die, who is buried in Chester, Pennsylvania, just outside Philadelphia. I will never forget Jerry's motherly former coworker, upon hearing we were heading later to Chester, tell us that we really did not want to go there, potentially for our own safety. We insisted it was all in the name of history.

I'm pretty sure the tour was scheduled for the afternoon, 3 or 4 pm, and that would be the only time the burial ground would be open. I learned later that there was a large restoration project underway at the burial ground that had it closed from 1997 to 2003. Today if one wanted to visit, it is open to the public seasonally during regular business hours. A lot of work was needed, as far as landscaping and stone conservation. According to a guidebook of the Burial Ground, about 4,000 people were buried in the yard, but only about 1,300 markers exist today. A survey was done in 1864 to record the markers at that time, but the guidebook says about 80% of the inscriptions have disappeared due to acid rain.[120] With those figures, imagine how many people rest here completely unidentified.

Unidentified graves were not just for the less prominent citizens of Philadelphia. A book about the Christ Church Burial Ground says records indicate that grave markers were not identified for three of the Declaration signers there: Francis Hopkinson, Joseph Hewes, and George Ross. Today there are small stones with modern brass markers to honor these men, but they do not necessarily mark the exact location of the remains. In the case of Hopkinson, three generations of the family are buried there according to the records, with one daughter's marker identified. Hopkinson's stone was placed nearby.[121]

The University of Pennsylvania Archives website mentions that Hopkinson's grave was not marked after his 1791 death. In the 1930s,

---

120 Wolf, *Lives of the Silent Stones in the Christ Church Burial Ground: 50 Family Profiles*, 3.

121 Wolf, *Lives of the Silent Stones in the Christ Church Burial Ground: 50 Family Profiles*, 28.

Hopkinson's descendants agreed to look for his remains by digging up his presumed plot. A piece of a skeleton was sent to the University of Pennsylvania and identified as Hopkinson, so his gravesite was finally marked.[122]

Fig 41: Francis Hopkinson's stone, Christ Church Burial Ground, Philadelphia, Pennsylvania

Francis Hopkinson was known as more than a politician. He was a writer, an artist, a musician, and a humorist. According to B.J. Lossing, who wrote in 1848,

HIS PEN WAS NOT DISTINGUISHED FOR DEPTH, BUT THERE WAS A GENUINE HUMOR IN HIS PRODUCTIONS, WHICH MADE HIM WIDELY POPULAR. A MAJORITY OF HIS

---

122 "Francis Hopkinson, 1737-1791," on archives.upenn.edu/exhibits/penn-people/ biography/francis-hopkinson, accessed on February 23, 2019, https://archives.upenn. edu/exhibits/penn-people/biography/francis-hopkinson.

POETICAL EFFUSIONS WERE OF AN EPHEMERAL NATURE,
AND WERE FORGOTTEN IN A DEGREE, WITH THE OCCASION
WHICH CALLED THEM FORTH; YET A FEW HAVE BEEN
PRESERVED, AMONG WHICH MAY BE MENTIONED "THE
BATTLE OF THE KEGS," A BALLAD, OR SORT OF EPIC, OF
INIMITABLE HUMOR.[123]

Hewes and Ross both died in 1779, with no markers listed for either one. Hewes, from North Carolina, died while serving in the Continental Congress. Years later, in 1894, North Carolina decided to reinter its three Declaration signers in a grave on the Guilford Courthouse battlefield. William Hooper and John Penn were moved from their original burial places, but Hewes' remains could not be found. The memorial at the park in North Carolina, dedicated in 1897, honors all three signers, but indicates that "Hewes' grave is lost. He was the third signer."[124]

Joseph Hewes was born a Quaker in New Jersey, but eventually moved to Edenton, North Carolina. He left the church when he realized that war was likely in the colonies, and also because he enjoyed dancing and the ladies, though he never married. His fiancée died just before their wedding.[125] While not in favor at first, Hewes was eventually convinced to vote for independence. John Adams described it dramatically:

MR. HEWES, WHO HAD HITHERTO CONSTANTLY VOTED

---

123 Lossing, *Lives of the Signers of the Declaration of Independence*, 86.

124 Thomas E. Baker, *The Monuments at Guilford Courthouse National Military Park* (1991), 47.

125 Memory F. Mitchell, *North Carolina's Signers: Brief Sketches of the Men Who Signed the Declaration of Independence and the Constitution.* (Raleigh, NC: State Department of Archives and History, 1964), 5.

AGAINST IT, STARTED SUDDENLY UPRIGHT, AND LIFTING UP BOTH OF HIS HANDS TO HEAVEN, AS IF HE HAD BEEN IN A TRANCE, CRIED OUT, "IT IS DONE! AND I WILL ABIDE BY IT."[126]

Hewes worked long hours in Congress, which may have led to his death at age 49.[127]

Fig 42: Joseph Hewes' stone, Christ Church Burial Ground, Philadelphia, Pennsylvania

George Ross, like Hewes, also died at age 49 in 1779. During his career, he was more involved in state matters and served a short time at the Continental Congress. He arrived after the momentous vote in July 1776, but in time to sign the Declaration on August 2. A popular story says that in 1776, George Ross, with George Washington and Robert Morris, visited Ross' nephew's wife, Betsy, to discuss making a new flag with stars and stripes.[128]

---

126   Mitchell, *North Carolina's Signers: Brief Sketches of the Men Who Signed the Declaration of Independence and the Constitution,* 7.

127   Mitchell, *North Carolina's Signers: Brief Sketches of the Men Who Signed the Declaration of Independence and the Constitution,* 7.

128   "Betsy Ross House: The Flag," on historicphiladelphia.org/betsy-ross-house/flag, accessed on February 24, 2019, http://historicphiladelphia.org/betsy-ross-house/flag/.

Fig 43: George Ross' stone, Christ Church Burial Ground,
Philadelphia, Pennsylvania

There is one more signer buried in the Christ Church Burial Ground: Benjamin Rush, who died in 1813, leaving a long resume. He was a physician who provided many theories on the transmission of diseases, which may not prove accurate today, but helped advance medical studies in the early nation. He cared for those with psychiatric problems and helped create various educational institutions. He supported abolition of slaves, the temperance movement, and public education.[129] My personal favorite accomplishment of his was getting Jefferson and Adams to communicate with each other after years of estrangement.[130] Rush's grave can be found along the east wall, with other members of his family.

---

129 Ferris, *Signers of the Declaration: Historic Places Commemorating the Signing of the Declaration*, 126.

130 McCullough, *John Adams*, 600.

Fig 44: Benjamin Rush's grave, Christ Church Burial Ground,
Philadelphia, Pennsylvania

I have returned to Christ Church Burial Ground many times over the years. With each visit I hope to learn more about the signers buried there, especially after discovering so many bizarre stories of signers' graves being moved. Now it is not just a matter of finding the grave, but questioning whether the signer is really buried in that location. I began my most recent visit to Philadelphia's cemetery by asking the young woman there if she could confirm for me that all five signers were actually buried in the yard. She was pretty confident in her answer, that yes, all five were in the yard. No doubt really about Franklin and Rush; both Benjamins were buried right where they remain today. Apparently Ross and Hewes were buried in the yard, but with no identifying markers, so they could be anywhere. Hopkinson was originally buried closer to Franklin, but the conditions deteriorated, and he was moved to the middle of the yard.

Five signers' graves in one yard. This was impressive, but Jerry and I were not done yet. We also went that day to Christ Church, where members of the Continental Congress worshipped. Two Declaration signers are buried just outside the church building. One is that of Robert Morris, not to be confused with Lewis Morris from New York who will be discussed later. Robert Morris was considered the financier of the American Revolution, responsible for raising funds to keep the Continental army going. Ironically, he eventually ended up in debtor's prison for overextending his own funds and died penniless. He is buried in a family vault, just behind the Christ Church that he once shared with William White, his brother-in-law.[131] White, who served as rector of the church and the first Episcopal Bishop of Pennsylvania, was later reburied inside the church.[132]

Fig 45: Robert Morris' grave, Christ Churchyard, Philadelphia, Pennsylvania

131 "Robert Morris," on dsdi1776.com/signers-by-state/robert-morris, accessed on March 16, 2019, https://www.dsdi1776.com/signers-by-state/robert-morris/.

132 "William White" on findagrave.com, accessed on March 16, 2019, https://www.findagrave.com/memorial/7596840/william-white.

The last grave we visited in Philadelphia that day was that of James Wilson, another one of the signers whose reputation slightly suffers due to the musical *1776*. Originally from Scotland, Wilson came to Pennsylvania and studied law, working at early law schools, serving in the Continental Congress and the Constitutional Convention, and eventually serving on the Supreme Court.[133] In the musical, however, he is the Pennsylvania delegate who sits in John Dickinson's shadow, constantly seconds his colony's own motions, and is the last representative to decide the question of American independence. While Pennsylvania's delegation did have to do some maneuvering, the decision did not fall solely into James Wilson's hands as the musical portrays. Pennsylvania's delegation was split on whether to vote for independence. Some members who did not support the resolution chose to stay away on the day of the vote, allowing Pennsylvania to join with the majority in favor of independence. Wilson does have an interesting story, as we found out after visiting his grave.

Wilson is buried just outside the Christ Church in Philadelphia, literally against the outside wall of the building. On the stone it identifies Wilson as a signer of the Declaration, the Constitution, and member of the Supreme Court. It says when he was born and when he died. Then it says "On November 22, 1906, the Governor and people of Pennsylvania removed

Fig 46: James Wilson's grave, Christ Churchyard, Philadelphia, Pennsylvania

133 Ferris, *Signers of the Declaration: Historic Places Commemorating the Signing of the Declaration*, 145-148.

his remains to Christ Church, Philadelphia and dedicated this tablet to his memory."

So here was another instance of a signer moved from his original burial place. While now I have come to expect this to be true, in the early days of the search, this was still a new phenomenon. This would require some additional research, and maybe another road trip, which is exactly what I did. My day with Jerry in Philadelphia was not quite finished yet, but let me take a detour here to finish up the James Wilson story.

In January of 2001, my friend Michael and I took a short trip down to North and South Carolina to do some history sightseeing and some signer research. The first stop was Edenton, North Carolina, the home of one signer, Joseph Hewes, and the place of death of another. In 1798, James Wilson was serving on the Supreme Court, yet suffering from serious debt. He traveled down to Edenton to visit his good friend and fellow justice James Iredell.[134] Wilson's health may have been in question as a result of his business troubles, and he may have used his circuit court travels as an excuse to get away from creditors and leave town.

Most sources say Wilson died at his friend Iredell's house in August 1798. So while visiting Edenton we decided to investigate the James Wilson story. Not only are the burial stories interesting, but in some cases, even the death story has some controversy to it. We woke up early and were on the front porch of the Edenton Visitor Center when they opened the doors that morning, eager to learn all we could about Wilson and his time in Edenton. It was unseasonably warm for January in North Carolina, so we decided to take the two-hour walking tour of the town, which included a stop at the Iredell house. I figured I would be able to see the room where Wilson died. Our tour guide was eager to answer

---

134 Ferris, *Signers of the Declaration: Historic Places Commemorating the Signing of the Declaration*, 148.

any questions. She explained the Iredell house had gone through changes over the years; some parts had been removed and replaced.

While upstairs I finally had a chance to ask about James Wilson's death. I was shocked to hear that he did not die in the house, but in a nearby tavern named Horniblow's. James Iredell was out of town, or arrived back around the time of Wilson's death, and documents show Wilson, at the time of his death, owed the Horniblows a large sum of money. Hannah Wilson, James' much younger wife, had come south to comfort her husband through his illness and would remain in Edenton, staying with the Iredells for many months following Wilson's death.

Now I wondered why so many sources claim that Wilson died at the Iredell home. How did an event like that get recorded wrong? As we walked out of the Iredell house, our guide pointed out a plaque on the chimney, claiming this was the site of James Wilson's death. The Daughters of the American Revolution put the plaque up in 1916. Why would they put the plaque there if he did not die there? The explanation seems to be that this was where the DAR wanted to put the plaque. Was a tavern not an appropriate location for a good patriot to spend his final hours? Sure makes one wonder how accurately history has been passed down to us.

Fig 47: James Wilson's plaque at the James Iredell House, Edenton, North Carolina

As we continued our walking tour, our guide pointed out the location of the Horniblow Tavern, long gone but situated next to the historic courthouse. We even found a drawing of the tavern in a display in the museum. The Horniblows owned slaves, one of whom was Harriet Jacobs, who wrote a well-known account of her experiences as a slave. We also visited St. Paul's Episcopal Church, dating back to 1736 with a graveyard including the stone for Charles Eden for whom the town is named. Outside the churchyard is a historical marker for Samuel Johnston, a governor of North Carolina and Iredell's brother-in-law. His burial spot is in a graveyard at the Hayes Plantation, one mile southeast, which was also where James Wilson was originally buried. We asked our guide about possibly visiting the Hayes Plantation. She explained it was on private property in a gated community, but she had been there before. It might be possible to walk out there. I promised her I would keep her name out of it if we found ourselves there.

I tend to be pretty honest and am not the biggest risk-taker, but we were so close to this old cemetery and it really needed to be done to complete the James Wilson story. We found the gate and were able to walk around it. We followed the road a short distance and found the cemetery not too far off the road. We snapped some photos and were on our way, excited to have found this original signer burial site. I admit to being a little nervous whenever a car went by.

Fig 48: James Wilson's original gravesite, Edenton,
North Carolina

I cannot say enough nice things about the folks at the Historic Edenton Visitor Center, who not only provided the tour and answered my
questions, but also gave me great resources to help with this project.
They copied for me an article from the *Journal of Supreme Court History*
by David W. Maxey, which details James Wilson's move from the Hayes
Plantation in Edenton to Christ Church in Philadelphia in 1906.[135]
What could serve as the impetus for moving Wilson's remains 108
years after his death?

In 1798, Wilson's death was not mentioned much in the Philadelphia
newspapers. But years later, as America entered the modern era, people
looked back to the ideals of the founding fathers, even if those fathers
weren't so perfect. Wilson's reputation was rejuvenated and improved
by an 1896 novel in which he appeared as a compassionate tutor to a
young Quaker patriot. After the American Revolution, the novel's main
character looks back at the Christ Church as the honored resting place

---

135   David W. Maxey, "The Translation of James Wilson," *Journal of Supreme Court History
1990* (1990), 33.

for national heroes such as Benjamin Franklin and Benjamin Rush. But his mentor James Wilson was not found there.[136]

The novel, *Hugh Wynne: Free Quaker*, was written by a Philadelphia physician named S. Weir Mitchell. Mitchell went to the University of Pennsylvania Law School dean, proposing the reinterment of Wilson's remains, citing evidence from someone in Edenton that Wilson lay in an unmarked grave there. Mitchell wrote that the letters received from Edenton "identify, without doubt the situation and present neglect of one of the greatest men Pennsylvania can claim as her own."[137]

Mitchell's comments seem a bit exaggerated in reference to James Wilson. People of Wilson's generation barely acknowledged his death. Had he lived, he may have been impeached while serving on the Supreme Court, having already served time for his financial troubles; this does not strike one as characteristics of "one of the greatest men Pennsylvania can claim as her own." With the passing of time, James Wilson might have his day.

The law school dean put a proposal together, expecting nothing would happen. Two others would get on board though, creating a James Wilson Memorial Committee that planned an elaborate ceremony to reinter Wilson's body. Rev. Burton Alva Konkle, originally from the Midwest, moved to Pennsylvania and dedicated his life to promoting Pennsylvania's history. His partner on the project was lawyer Lucien H. Alexander.[138] These men even paid a visit to President Theodore Roosevelt, inviting him to participate in the event. Roosevelt declined ironically, because he had recently participated in another colonial-era reinterment—that of naval hero John Paul Jones who was reburied in Annapolis, Maryland,

---

136 Maxey, "The Translation of James Wilson," 33.

137 Maxey, "The Translation of James Wilson," 34.

138 Maxey, "The Translation of James Wilson," 34.

after years in France. There were some definite political undertones in these events, as politicians could use these occasions to promote their agendas while highlighting these historic figures.[139]

Wilson had quite a show in November 1906. A group of dignitaries went to Edenton to fetch his remains. I thought folks in Edenton said Wilson's grave was unmarked. How did they find his remains? Did they really reinter the remains of James Wilson? In any case, the Secretary of the Navy provided the USS *Dubuque* to carry Wilson's remains to Philadelphia. Wilson's casket had the honor to lay in the historic east room at Independence Hall, where Wilson had debated the Declaration of Independence and the Constitution. The public paid their respects for a few hours before Wilson's body was carried four blocks to Christ Church.[140] Speakers at the ceremony included Pennsylvania Gov. Samuel Pennypacker, Chief Justice of the Supreme Court Melville Fuller, Supreme Court Justice Edward White, Attorney General William Moody, author S. Weir Mitchell, and Andrew Carnegie, who shared a Scottish heritage with Wilson. After all the speeches, Wilson was laid to rest outside Christ Church. Rev. Konkle wrote the inscription on the headstone, sending an identical stone to Edenton. The date on the stone, however, was a week off from the date Wilson died. By the end of this project Konkle and Alexander, who had worked together to make the reburial and elaborate ceremony happen, disliked each other, feeling each deserved more credit for the event.[141]

How many people walk by the headstone of James Wilson in the Christ Churchyard in Philadelphia and never realize all that happened to get Wilson there? After some of the stories I have heard, I may still

---

139 Maxey, "The Translation of James Wilson," 35.
140 Maxey, "The Translation of James Wilson," 38.
141 Maxey, "The Translation of James Wilson," 40.

wonder if Wilson's remains made that journey from Edenton, but it certainly makes for an interesting addition to the signers' graves collection. Let's return to that day in August of 2000, when Jerry and I spent the day photographing the two graves at the Christ Churchyard and the five stones in the Christ Church Burial Ground down the street. Not to be greedy, because seven in one day would be the all-time high for one day of graving, but there was still hope for one more. John Morton, the first of the signers to die, lived in suburban Philadelphia and according to findagrave.com was buried in Chester, Pennsylvania. We thought we could make a quick stop in Chester on our way home. As mentioned earlier, Chester did not have the safest reputation, as evidenced by Jerry's former coworker telling us not to go there. But we were confident we could find the churchyard we were looking for, snap the photo, and be safely on our way. Sometimes the best plans do not work out.

The only information I had on John Morton's grave was from findagrave.com, which said Morton was buried at Saint Paul's Church in Chester. That August day, we found Saint Paul's Church at 9th and Madison streets. We drove around every angle of that building and found no burial ground anywhere nearby. Having been to many a churchyard in search of the signers, I know that often the burial ground and the church are not that close together—earlier that day we were in Philadelphia, where the church building and burial ground are blocks apart. After a long day of graving, and admittedly being in a sketchy area as the day ended, we decided to save John Morton for another day and head home. It was incredibly frustrating to be so close, yet not be able to find what we were looking for. As we drove home though, we could reflect back on a big day for the grave hunt—seven signers' graves had been found which was pretty impressive. John Morton would have to wait for another trip.

XIV

The Lees of Virginia

O ne of the more ironic parts of my search was that often the graves closest to my location in Washington, DC were the most difficult to find. Such was the case with the Lee brothers, the only set of brothers to sign the Declaration. Both were buried in Virginia, the state I live in, and both were slightly off the beaten path.

My search for Richard Henry Lee began one day when I was out by myself exploring. I had just gone out for a drive to see if I could find Lee's grave. I had very little information to go on, which I had found on findagrave.com—just that he was buried in the small town of Hague, Virginia, on the Northern Neck along the Potomac. I had no name of a church or specific information of any kind. I guessed I was heading out to what was once the Lee family property. In fact, I wasn't far from Stratford Hall, another Lee family homestead. The father of Richard Henry and Francis Lightfoot, the signers, had built Stratford Hall. Today it is most well-known as the birthplace of Robert E. Lee, Confederate general during the Civil War. This is a tricky family to keep in order, but in case one is interested, the signers' brother Philip Ludwell Lee's daughter Matilda married her cousin Light Horse Harry Lee. Matilda died, leaving the home to Harry, who married Ann Carter, who gave birth to Robert E. Lee at Stratford Hall.[142]

Why I didn't think to call Stratford Hall for clarification, I am not sure. I figured this would be an adventure, and hopefully easy enough to check another signer's name off the list. Silly me. I was enjoying my drive on Virginia Route 202 through the small town of Hague, which I later learned was where my boss grew up. I should have thought to ask him for directions. This is a pretty rural area, so I was really excited to find a state historical marker on the side of the road. "A mile and a half north, in the Lee burying ground, is the grave of Richard Henry Lee, who died June 19, 1794." I thought I was in good shape. I was only a mile and a half away. Not having a compass or ever remembering which way the sun rises or sets, I continued on the current route, looking for the Lee burying ground. When I had gone further than a few miles, I turned around, figuring I must have driven past it. Another drive down the same stretch of road, and no luck. There was a general store in town, and I don't remember much more than that. I think I stopped for a moment to contemplate my next move, but I don't even think I asked anyone there for directions. I was pretty determined that I was going to find Richard Henry Lee's grave myself.

---

142 Alonzo T. Dill and Mary Tyler Cheek, *A Visit to Stratford and the Story of the Lees* (Richmond, VA: W.M. Brown and Son Printing Company, 1986), 52.

Fig 49: Historical marker for Richard Henry Lee's grave, Hague, Virginia

The musical, *1776*, which is partly responsible for setting me out on this quest, portrays Richard Henry Lee unfairly. Historically, he is the member of the Continental Congress who provides the resolution on independence, a major step toward the colonies separating from Great Britain.[143] As much as I love the musical, Lee comes across as a bumbling character, who ends all his phrases with "Lee" in order to show how prominent his family is to the Virginia colony. His song about his famous family is amusing, but does a slight disservice to his memory. Yet while out there in rural Virginia looking for his remains, all I could think of was that song, and how every time I watch the movie I feel bad for the poor horse that the actor jumps on and off of while singing about the Lees. As I drove up and down that Virginia state highway, I was getting more and more frustrated and finally gave up, unsuccessful in my mission and determined to figure out where that grave could be.

---

143   Paul C. Nagel, *The Lees of Virginia: Seven Generations of an American Family* (New York: Oxford University Press, 1990), 5.

This Lee situation had me very perturbed. Not that I had traveled that far from home, but that I was so close and couldn't figure out where the grave was located. It finally occurred to me to call Stratford Hall, the historic site that tells the Lee family story. Surely they would know where Lee's grave was—and while I was at it, there was that other brother to ask about too.

My call to Stratford Hall was very illuminating. The folks there were able to give me great directions to Richard Henry's grave, which I had been really close to on my first trip. They also provided information about Francis Lightfoot's grave, which now falls on private property. I explained my project and asked about the possibility of visiting. The person I talked to could give no guarantees, but gave me the name of the home's owner, a Mrs. Tayloe. This was amazing to me—Francis Lightfoot married Rebecca Tayloe—the house was still in the family! Coming from a family that has barely been in this country a century, these long-time connections are fascinating. Living near Washington, DC, I have visited the Octagon House, which was built by the Tayloe family.[144]

After such a successful day of graving in Philadelphia, Jerry was willing to join me for another fun day the following week. We were off to visit some really interesting sites.

Let's start with Richard Henry Lee. That frustrating trip to the Northern Neck would be forgotten (well, maybe not totally) after I finally found this Lee grave. After passing that historic marker, we turned down a dirt road, wondering if we could possibly be in the right place. I don't recall any signs to point us in the right direction, but we kept down this dirt road driving through a cornfield. Just when we thought we must be in the wrong place and were ready to go back, we rounded a corner

---

144 "History," on architectsfoundation.org/octagon-museum/history, accessed on March 2, 2019, https://architectsfoundation.org/octagon-museum/history/.

and there was this brick wall enclosing a small burial ground. It was the strangest thing I had ever seen. We were driving through this cornfield and literally turned the corner to find this brick wall. I realize I may be repeating myself, but it was that unusual. We got out and walked into a small family graveyard. It was definitely one of the more unique graves I found on the search.

Fig 50: Burnt House Field, Hague, Virginia

The Lee family called this the Burnt House Field, because they had a house nearby that burned down and was apparently never rebuilt in that location.[145] I found a great article from a Richmond newspaper in 1938, which talked about this "apparently forgotten tomb" in honor of a founding father. "That grave in the field of waving corn holds the dust of the man who wrote the resolutions adopted by the Continental Congress declaring the colonies to be thenceforth free of the rule of Great Britain."[146] Just as I was surprised by the condition of many signers' graves, this article cited a drama teacher, Miss Mary Olive O'Connell,

---

145 Nagel, *The Lees of Virginia: Seven Generations of an American Family*, 46.

146 James Grotius, "Richard Henry Lee's Grave in Cornfield," *Richmond Times-Dispatch*, September 25, 1938.

who was unsettled by Richard Henry Lee's hard-to-find grave. She was even moved to poetry:

DEEP-HIDDEN FROM THE CASUALLY CURIOUS
BY PROTECTING ROWS OF STATELY CORN
IS THE FORGOTTEN GRAVE OF AN AMERICAN HERO.
HIGH BRICK WALLS WITHHOLD THE ENCROACHING WEEDS
THAT SEEK TO SMOTHER THE SACRED TOMB
WHEREIN LIES STATEMAN RICHARD HENRY LEE
BENEATH THE SOIL HE LOVED AND FOUGHT FOR
NEAREST THE HEART OF HIS FATHERS' LAND.
SILENT NOW THE MOUTH THAT SHOUTED—FREEDOM!
STILLED THE HAND THAT SIGNED A MIGHTY DOCUMENT
SLEEPS 'TIL ETERNITY A FATHER OF OUR INDEPENDENCE.
HAS THEN THE STAR SO LOWLY FALLEN
FROM HEIGHTS OF GLORY TO A COMMON CORNFIELD?
HAS MEMORY GROWN SO DIM OR LIFE SO FURIOUS
THAT TOWARD THIS QUIET SPOT NO PATH IS WORN?
BUT STAY—IS NOT DIGNITY WITHIN THESE WALLS,
AND PEACE, FAR FROM THE SPEED-MAD HIGHWAY
IS IT, PERHAPS, MORE FIT THAT HERE,
CLOSE TO THE MUSIC OF THE CHANGING SEASONS,
DEEP-HIDDEN FROM THE CASUALLY CURIOUS
BY PROTECTING ROWS OF STATELY CORN
LIES THE FORGOTTEN GRAVE OF AN AMERICAN HERO?[147]

---

147 James Grotius, "Richard Henry Lee's Grave in Cornfield," *Richmond Times-Dispatch*. September 25, 1938.

I revisited Richard Henry Lee's grave in early 2012. Even though I knew what it would look like, to suddenly come upon this old brick enclosure in the midst of an open field, surprised me again and made me thankful that those before me understood the value of historic preservation in saving this special site.

Fig 51 and 52: Burnt House Field and Richard Henry Lee's grave, Hague, Virginia

While Richard Henry Lee gets the glory in the musical *1776*, or at least the funny song about the Lees of Virginia, he was not the only member of the family to sign the Declaration. Francis Lightfoot Lee also signed, making them the only pair of brothers to sign the document. Francis' place in history appears less well-known than Richard's, but both supported the patriot cause. As someone who lives in Northern Virginia, it is interesting that Francis Lightfoot Lee was an early representative to Loudoun County and property owner of land that now makes up Dulles Airport.[148]

After making the call to Stratford Hall, I decided to call the Tayloes and see how receptive the family was to sharing the great history on their property. I was fortunate to find the number and talk with Mrs. Tayloe

148   Nagel, *The Lees of Virginia: Seven Generation of an American Family*, 68.

regarding my search. I will never forget how the conversation began. I explained what I was doing, looking for all the signers' graves, and asked about the possibility of coming by for a photograph. The first thing she said to me was, "I hope you don't mind cattle!" I was taken aback by that, not knowing exactly how to respond. I'm sure I was already nervous, calling up a stranger and asking if I could come to her home. She went on to tell me that the Lee graves were out in a cow pasture, so I was welcome to come by, as long as I understood what I was getting into. I was so eager for the opportunity, that it didn't occur to me that I wasn't the biggest fan of cows. But as my friends will say, when getting me to do things I don't like, it is all in the name of history. And what a great opportunity this would be to visit a site not open to the public and add another grave to the collection.

I made an appointment with Mrs. Tayloe to visit Mount Airy, the plantation home in Warsaw, Virginia. She was very gracious to us, and even showed us around the first floor of the house. I was so impressed by the fact that it looked like a historic site that one would go to visit, like a Monticello, for instance, but yet it had a lived-in atmosphere. This was one of those days that I was really thankful for getting into this project, because this was such a unique experience to have a descendant of the family showing us around her home. She led us out the back door and pointed off in the direction of the family cemetery. She probably warned us again about the cows we might run into as we made the trek through the field. We were up for the challenge, although it was a bit of an adventure.

I will never forget Jerry that day, who was wearing a shirt his future wife had gotten him. It was a bright color, what I would consider pink. It was August and very hot. We were out in a field, climbing between fences, trying to avoid the cows and their droppings, and most of all, swatting at

Fig 53: Jerry climbing through the fence, Mount Airy Plantation, Warsaw, Virginia

mosquitoes. I really remember the mosquitoes. What we do for history. We crossed the field and made our way to this small family graveyard and found the grave of Francis Lightfoot Lee. The headstone looked fairly recent and until later, when I would see the trend in reburying the signers, it did not occur to me that maybe this was not his original burial place. After all, this house had clearly been in the family a very long time. We made our way back through the field, ducking between the barbed-wire fence and still avoiding the cows. I don't think the cows were any more eager to get close to us than we were to them. The mosquitoes were another story. They were pretty fierce that day. We got back to the house and thanked Mrs. Tayloe again for the privilege of letting us visit, not only the family graveyard, but also her home. It was a very special day in the search for the signers.

Fig 54: Mount Airy family cemetery, Warsaw, Virginia

Fig 55: Francis Lightfoot Lee's grave, Mount Airy, Warsaw, Virginia

The day was not over yet, however. Two Lee graves found, but Virginia had one more for us to find that day. Before leaving the Lees behind, though, let me finish up the Francis Lightfoot Lee story. Years later, in

2012, my friend Bert and I would visit the remains of Francis Lightfoot Lee's home, known as Menokin, not all that far from Mount Airy. With no children, Francis and Rebecca's home fell to a nephew, then changed hands numerous times, eventually falling into disrepair. The Menokin Foundation took on responsibility for the property in 1995. Instead of trying to restore the house to its colonial look, the foundation has left it in its current state in order to teach about historic preservation. Today one sees the beams and the interior which are usually not visible at a historic home that is pristinely preserved.[149]

While at Menokin, Bert and I met a historian who filled us in briefly on the Lees. Both Francis Lightfoot and Rebecca died in 1797, just ten days apart, and were originally buried nearby. One source called it a local parish graveyard.[150] As the property passed out of the family, and with concern for erosion by the Rappahannock River nearby, the Lees' graves were moved to Mount Airy about thirty years later.[151] Hence the rather recent date on the headstone at Mount Airy. This then adds to the list of signers who were moved from their original burial spot to the location where they currently rest. How exactly a move like that happens years later, I am still not clear. But this seems to be quite a trend in the burial stories of the signers of the Declaration of Independence. I also learned that the very helpful Mrs. Tayloe had recently passed away. I have such fond memories of that day and am so grateful for her kindness in sharing her historic property with us. Upon further research, it appears the family still lives in the home and occasionally offers it up for events.

Let's return to that August day when Jerry and I were exploring Virginia's history. Fired up after a very exciting trip to both Lee graves,

---

149 "Story of the House" on menokin.org/our-story/story-of-the-house, accessed on March 3, 2019, www.menokin.org/our-story/story-of-the-house/.

150 Nagel, *The Lees of Virginia*, 142.

151 Nagel, *The Lees of Virginia*, 142.

Jerry and I were not finished yet. I was still missing the grave of Thomas Nelson, Jr., who was buried in Yorktown, Virginia. It seemed fairly easy to continue along the Northern Neck and make our way to Yorktown to pay our respects to Colonel Nelson. Having worked at Colonial National Historical Park and visited Yorktown as a child, I remember seeing the Nelson house on the Yorktown tour, with the cannonball in the wall. A Revolutionary War story tells of Colonel Nelson ordering the troops to fire on his own house for the sake of the cause.[152] But I had never thought to look for his grave before.

Since we were on such a roll, we moved on to Yorktown and found the grave of Thomas Nelson, Jr. in the yard of the Grace Episcopal Church. This was a big change from the Tayloe family cow pasture. Another element that has made this search so interesting is the variety of places I have gone to find the signers. Little did I know, as I wandered through the Grace Churchyard, what a sad story befell Colonel Nelson.

Fig 56 and 57: Thomas Nelson, Jr.'s grave, Grace Episcopal
Churchyard, Yorktown, Virginia

152   Emory G. Evans, *Thomas Nelson of Yorktown: Revolutionary Virginian* (Williamsburg, VA: The Colonial Williamsburg Foundation, 1975), 119.

Not only was Nelson a signer of the Declaration, but he served in the Revolutionary War and as governor of Virginia. When he died at the age of 50 in 1789, he had no money. His family buried him in an unmarked grave, right near his father's grave, so that people whom Nelson owed money would not try and use his body as collateral for getting paid.[153] At one point, a website no longer live called Remember Yorktown claimed that Nelson's headstone was placed in the yard between 1913 and 1920 and that the dates of birth and death on the stone are incorrect. Here is another example of a signer who gave his all for the cause and yet was treated so sadly in death.

A tribute from Colonel Innis on the death of Thomas Nelson appears on the Colonial Hall biography website:

THE ILLUSTRIOUS GENERAL THOMAS NELSON IS NO MORE! HE PAID THE LAST GREAT DEBT TO NATURE, ON SUNDAY, THE FOURTH OF THE PRESENT MONTH, AT HIS ESTATE IN HANOVER. HE WHO UNDERTAKES BARELY TO RECITE THE EXALTED VIRTUES WHICH ADORNED THE LIFE OF THIS GREAT AND GOOD MAN, WILL UNAVOIDABLY PRONOUNCE A PANEGYRIC ON HUMAN NATURE. AS A MAN, A CITIZEN, A LEGISLATOR, AND A PATRIOT, HE EXHIBITED A CONDUCT UNTARNISHED AND UNDEBASED BY SORDID OR SELFISH INTEREST, AND STRONGLY MARKED WITH THE GENUINE CHARACTERISTICS OF TRUE RELIGION, SOUND BENEVOLENCE, AND LIBERAL POLICY. ENTERTAINING THE MOST ARDENT LOVE FOR CIVIL AND RELIGIOUS LIBERTY, HE WAS AMONG THE FIRST OF THAT GLORIOUS BAND OF PATRIOTS WHOSE

---

153 "Brigadier General Thomas Nelson Jr," on nps.gov/york/learn/historyculture/ nelsonjrbio, accessed on March 17, 2019, https://www.nps.gov/york/learn/ historyculture/nelsonjrbio.htm.

EXERTIONS DASHED AND DEFEATED THE MACHINATIONS OF
BRITISH TYRANNY, AND GAVE UNITED AMERICA FREEDOM
AND INDEPENDENT EMPIRE.[154]

One would think a man deserving of such a eulogy would receive better in death. Even after finding so many sad signer death stories, I am still so surprised by the great number of these brave men who met such tragic endings.

The day was still not over. Jerry and I had one more stop. In the continuing trend of grave hunting and baseball games, we made our way down to Norfolk and caught a Tidewater Tides minor league baseball game. It was a long ride home that night to Northern Virginia, but that gave us plenty of time to reflect on the great history we had experienced that day and recover from all the mosquito bites we got while hiking through the cow pasture. It is all about the history.

XV

Back to PA

I was on quite a roll that summer of 2000, finding ten graves in two weeks. I was very motivated to keep this streak alive. After the struggle to find John Morton in Chester, Pennsylvania, I was extremely determined to figure out where Jerry and I had gone wrong. Luckily, I discovered my error fairly easily and convinced my friend Michael that a return trip to Pennsylvania was in order. Hearing the warnings about Chester from Jerry's ranger friend made me hesitant to take this trip alone. For some reason we joked that the fall always seems like a good time for Revolutionary War sites, so that October Michael and I were off to find John Morton.

Before we left, I tried to figure out how we could have been so lost on the first try. All became clear as I realized what Jerry and I found was St. Paul's Church in Chester on 9th and Madison streets. What we wanted to find was St. Paul's Churchyard, which was the site of the first St. Paul's Church, as far back as the late 1600s, according to the website oldchesterpa.com. The current church was built in about 1900. The burying ground was at Welsh Avenue and East 3rd Street, blocks away from today's church building. The historic marker in front refers to it as the Old Swedish Burial Ground. While either name seems acceptable, this yard marks where John Morton is buried, the first of the signers who died.[155]

On the north side of the monument over his grave is this quote:

"John Morton being censured by some of his friends for his boldness in giving his casting vote for the Declaration of Independence, his prophetic spirit dictated from his death bed the following message to them: 'Tell them they will live to see the hour when they shall acknowledge it to have been the most glorious service I ever rendered to my country."[156]

This quotation is a great reminder that while Declaration signers are viewed as heroes today, at the time they signed the document it was unknown whether they would be on the winning side. Opinions were split on whether separating from Great Britain was the right decision. Morton died in April 1777, never living to see the successful end of the Revolutionary War or realize his contribution. While this puts the signers' struggles in perspective, according to the website of the descendants of the signers, the quotation appeared in the 1900s and cannot be accurately attributed to Morton.[157] It serves as an interesting commentary of the times, before independence was a definite outcome.

---

155   "Old Chester, PA: Cemeteries: St. Paul's Burying Ground," on oldchesterpa.com/cemeteries/stpcemetery.htm, accessed on February 28, 2019, http://www.oldchesterpa.com/cemeteries/stpcemetery.htm.

156   "Old Chester, PA: Cemeteries: St. Paul's Burying Ground," on oldchesterpa.com/cemeteries/stpcemetery.htm, accessed on February 28, 2019, http://www.oldchesterpa.com/cemeteries/stpcemetery.htm.

157   "John Morton," on dsdi1776.com/signers-by-state/john-morton, accessed on February 28, 2019, www.dsdi1776.com/signers-by-state/john-morton/.

On that same weekend we also traveled to Hopewell, New Jersey, in search of John Hart. Locating his grave was fairly easy in the small downtown area. Hart is buried in the yard of the First Baptist Church, which was apparently built on land he donated. As I have said before, when I first started out on the search, it was all about taking the picture and checking a name off the list. I had no idea how many great stories I would find along the way. I was not concentrating on the research, nor thinking about how hard it might be to figure out all of the stories later. At this point, I would have taken the grave at face value, not even expecting there could be more to the story. So as I look again at John Hart, I am faced with another mystery.

Fig 58: John Morton's grave, St. Paul's Churchyard, Chester, Pennsylvania

According to a Hopewell, New Jersey, website, "Hopewell's illustrious citizen and patriot, John Hart, lies reburied in land he donated to the Old School Baptist Churchyard."[158] It is possible, as with many of these men, that he was buried on his own property and later moved. I can't find any history about the church building, except that the current building was built in 1822.[159] The shiny gold on the headstone says Hart died in 1780. The stone must be relatively new. It adds to the list of those who apparently do not rest in their original burial place.

---

158 "History and historic sites," on hopewellboro-nj.us/community/history-historic-sites, accessed on March 6, 2019, www.hopewellboro-nj.us/community/history-historic-sites/.

159 "History and historic sites," on hopewellboro-nj.us/community/history-historic-sites, accessed on March 6, 2019, www.hopewellboro-nj.us/community/history-historic-sites/.

I made contact with the Hopewell Museum by phone and inquired about John Hart's grave. The first thing the woman said when I asked about Hart's burial was, "You mean his reburial?" I immediately felt like I had hit the jackpot and would get the information that I was looking for regarding Hart. Beverly at the Hopewell Museum was very helpful in filling in the story.

Originally, Hart and his wife were buried in a family plot in Woodsville, New Jersey, about five miles from Hopewell. The property belonged to his wife's family. Deborah Scudder Hart died in October 1776. The Harts were one family that suffered at the hands of the British during the Revolutionary War. Legends have been passed down that Hart hid from the British in a nearby cave and came out of hiding to find his wife had died. His property was damaged and his health tested. He would continue to serve in the New Jersey Assembly, until he stepped down due to poor health. Hart also hosted General Washington and his army on his property before they went off to the Battle of Monmouth in 1778.[160]

Hart died on May 11, 1779, at his Hopewell home at age 68. In the May 19 edition of the *New Jersey Gazette*, an obituary included these comments:

"He had served in the Assembly for many years under the former government, taken an early and active part in the present revolution, and continued to the day he was seized with his last illness to discharge the duties of a faithful and upright patriot in the service of his country in general and the county he represented in particular."[161]

---

160 "John Hart," on revolutionarynj.org/rev-neighbors/john-hart, accessed on March 23, 2019, https://revolutionarynj.org/rev-neighbors/john-hart/.

161 "John Hart," on dsdi1776.com/signers-by-state/john-hart, accessed on March 6, 2019, www.dsdi1776.com/signers-by-state/john-hart/.

Fig 59 and 60: John Hart's grave, First Baptist Church, Hopewell, New Jersey

Beverly at the Hopewell Museum was not sure about markings at the original burial place. Years later, folks felt Hart deserved a more prominent burial location with a monument recognizing the spot. So he was moved from the family yard to the grounds of the Old School Baptist Church, today known as the First Baptist Church of Hopewell. This included land that once was owned by Hart, which he had donated for the community's use. Beverly mentioned that when they reburied him in downtown Hopewell, they left his wife's remains in the family yard. She thought members of the Daughters of the American Revolution had arranged a marker for Deborah Hart, which is located next to her husband's grave, even though her remains are miles away. I thought of Abigail Adams' famous line to her husband John about remembering the ladies. Deborah Hart may not have served in politics, but she certainly suffered the effects of the Revolution. Yet today she remains buried alone in a family cemetery, away from her husband who is prominently buried in the town.

Not being too far removed from the Roger Sherman or the Charles Thomson story, I had to call the Hopewell Museum back to ask one more question that I had forgotten to ask. Beverly explained the reburial had happened on July 4, 1865. "Everything happened on July 4," she told me. I found it pretty interesting that the year was 1865, as the Civil War ended. New Jersey Gov. Joel Parker was present to give the speech at the dedication of the new grave monument, connecting the country's recent events to this founding father. 86 years had passed since Hart's death. In cases where other signers had been reburied, there was sometimes a question of whether or not the remains really made it to the new burial spot. The call back to Beverly was to find out if people in Hopewell believe John Hart's remains really are under that new monument in the yard of the First Baptist Church.

The answer is yes. Apparently there are accounts existing from the time of the reburial documenting the witnesses who saw Hart's remains and that he was moved to the new location. Beverly even invited me to the Hopewell Museum to see a lock of Hart's hair that was likely gotten during this time period when the remains were transferred.

It is amazing to me that someone who died in 1779 could have anything recognizable in 1865. These signers' stories get more and more interesting as I continue on the search. Who knows what the next signer story will bring?

One more question still lingered about John Hart and necessitated another call to the Hopewell Museum, where I again spoke to Beverly. She remembered talking to me weeks earlier about Hart's reburial. While working on this chapter, I had flipped through my photo album of all the grave photos and noticed that Hart's date of death on the headstone said 1780. Most sources claim he died in 1779.

Beverly and the folks at the Hopewell Museum believe Hart died in 1779 based on their sources. It seems a pretty drastic typo to make and I didn't get a sense that they know why the stone says 1780. She thinks, based on the photos they have of the dedication in 1865, that the current stone in the cemetery was the stone placed there in 1865.

Before I leave John Hart, a few lines from Gov. Parker's speech at the dedication of the monument over Hart's newly placed remains in 1865:

AND NOW, MY FRIENDS, OUR DUTY IS PERFORMED, AND WE WILL SOON LEAVE THIS CONSECRATED GROUND. THIS MONUMENT MAY CRUMBLE BUT THE FAME OF HIM WHOSE REMAINS ARE ENTOMBED SHALL NEVER DIE. THE HISTORIC PAGE WILL SPEAK OF HIM TO POSTERITY. MAY WE NOT HOPE THAT, AFTER ALL NOW HERE ASSEMBLED SHALL HAVE PASSED FROM EARTH, IN THE FAR-OFF CENTURIES, FUTURE GENERATIONS SHALL STAND BY THIS TOMB, DEDICATED TO VIRTUE AND PATRIOTISM, AND AS THEY CONTEMPLATE THE CHARACTER OF WHOSE DUST LIES BENEATH THIS MONUMENT, DRAW INSPIRATION FROM THIS HALLOWED SPOT; AND HERE, BENEATH THE SHADOW OF THIS TEMPLE DEDICATED TO ALMIGHTY GOD, RENEW THEIR VOWS AND SWEAR THAT THIS WORK SHALL NEVER PERISH, AND THE UNION SHALL BE PERPETUAL?[162]

---

162 Abraham Van Doren Honeyman, editor, *The New Jersey Law Journal, Vol XXIII* (Plainfield, NJ: New Jersey Law Journal Publishing Company, 1900), 328.

XVI

Return to Laurel Hill

I was really consumed with this grave project and wanted to continue visiting those that I could find easily and were close by. I asked Michael if he was up for another Pennsylvania visit that fall of 2000 in order to find the grave of Thomas McKean. McKean represented Delaware in the Continental Congress, but later served as governor of Pennsylvania. It is thought that McKean was the last of the signers to sign the document, as he also served in the military and supposedly was not in Philadelphia in August of 1776, when most signed the Declaration. There also appeared to be a signed copy that did not include McKean's signature, which has led historians to conclude he must have signed it later. According to a descendant of McKean's, he left a letter that explained why his name wasn't on the first copy, but claims he was there in August to sign. It is not clear when exactly McKean signed, but many sources believe he was the last to put his name on the Declaration.[163]

McKean's grave was easy to find in Laurel Hill Cemetery. This is a beautiful historic cemetery right along the Schuylkill River in Philadelphia. It prides itself in the artistic headstones, as it was created during the Victorian era. Downtown Philadelphia was outgrowing its churchyard cemeteries and needed more space, so this land was set aside as a cemetery around 1836.[164]

Fig 61: Thomas McKean's grave, Laurel Hill Cemetery, Philadelphia, Pennsylvania

Thomas McKean died in 1817. I should have recognized right away that something did not make sense here when I first visited Laurel Hill. In those days though, I was eager to take the photograph and not give much thought to the story surrounding the signer and his burial. I was just glad to check another grave off the list. As I discovered more signers with unusual stories and dates that didn't add up, I have sometimes had to return to the scene and figure out what happened.

I was fortunate upon my return to Laurel Hill to meet with Carol Yaster, who would answer many of my questions and more. She had an unexpected story for me. When I approached her outside the cemetery office, I told her of my interest in the Declaration signers. She said, "We

163 "Thomas McKean," on dsdi1776.com/signers-by-state/thomas-mckean, accessed on June 10, 2019, www.dsdi1776.com/signers-by-state/thomas-mckean/.

164 "History," on thelaurelhillcemetery.org/about/history, accessed on March 23, 2019, https://thelaurelhillcemetery.org/about/history.

have two here maybe." I was obviously there to inquire about McKean, so I was not quite sure who else she meant, unless she was referring to Charles Thomson, the secretary of the Continental Congress. On my first visit to Laurel Hill, I found Thomson's grave in a beautiful spot overlooking the river. Thomson is not considered a signer, as he was the secretary and not a member of the Congress. His name does appear on the document with John Hancock's though from July 4, 1776.

Yaster assured me that Thomas McKean was buried here at Laurel Hill. After Roger Sherman in New Haven, I believe I will always be skeptical about those who have been reburied actually being in their new resting spots. Yaster was convincing, as she told me about McKean's original burial in the churchyard of the Second Presbyterian Church in Philadelphia. Eventually that church would close and move to another location, meaning all the burials in the churchyard had to be moved. It was around this time that Laurel Hill Cemetery opened. Cemeteries in downtown Philadelphia were too crowded as the city expanded. The idea of a rural cemetery was appealing. As planners for this new cemetery worked to get the city behind the project, they were looking for prominent supporters of Laurel Hill.

In the 1830s, the Declaration signers would still have been real heroes. Cemetery planners went to the McKean family, who were happy to have the former governor and his immediate family moved from the churchyard on Bank Street where he was originally buried to the new Laurel Hill Cemetery.

In one of the more memorable moments in this signer search, while chatting with Yaster, she walked back toward a records room to confirm McKean's original burial location. She reemerged with a folder of information about McKean, including the permit for interment at Laurel Hill, dated December 4, 1843. She let me hold the document and then made me a copy to take with me. It was so exciting to be holding a record so significant to this signers' search. She thought it very possible that McKean's reinterment could have happened with a lot of fanfare. Here was a family willing to support this new endeavor and proud to have McKean and his family resting in Laurel Hill.

This was not the case with Charles Thomson's family. Yaster shared with me the fascinating story of Thomson's possible reinterment at Laurel Hill. His descendants were not keen on moving Thomson's remains to Laurel Hill, preferring to keep him at his family home, Harriton, where he had died in 1824. The cemetery planners were persistent though and found one relative, a nephew, who was willing to make the move. The Harriton House website notes that graves in the family cemetery often were not identified with headstones in the Quaker tradition.[165] Apparently the removal of the Thomsons' bodies from the family yard was done under cover of darkness. The process was interrupted, with only three members of the family moved to Laurel Hill. No one is really sure which family members now rest there along the Schuylkill. When I asked Yaster her opinion, whether or not she thought Charles Thomson was there at Laurel Hill, she said she "didn't really have a horse in the race" and could not elaborate any further.

Though Thomson does not count as one of the 56 signers, after hearing the story of this burial, it was hard to leave him out of the book. After all, his name does appear on a copy of the Declaration even if it is only as a witness. Thomson is a little-known figure today, but was front and center as the nation began. He served as the secretary of the Continental Congress throughout its existence and followed through until the Constitution went into effect, at which time he retired from his position.

165 "Harriton Cemetery," on lowermerionhistory.org/burial/harriton, accessed on March 23, 2019, http://www.lowermerionhistory.org/burial/harriton/.

Imagine the conversations and debates he witnessed throughout the years. Thomson kept notes during his time with the Congress and worked on a history that would have been unique from his vantage point. Before he shared his work though, he reconsidered and feared shining a negative light on any of his colleagues.[166] Instead of sharing his recollections, he burned all of his notes, denying future generations a wonderful resource on the nation's origins. What a fascinating character to do such a thing, when many of his contemporaries were certainly considering how history would remember them. Here is another unexpected story along the way that I might not have discovered had it not been for this grave hunt. I am so lucky that I made a return trip to Laurel Hill on the day I did, meeting Yaster and learning about the creation of this amazing cemetery.

Fig 62: Charles Thomson's grave, Laurel Hill Cemetery, Philadelphia, Pennsylvania

---

166   "Patriot Charles Thomson," on uschs.wordpress.com/2013/07/23/patriot-charles-thomson, accessed on March 23, 2019, https://uschs.wordpress.com/2013/07/23/patriot-charles-thomson/.

XVII

Rhode Island

After great success in finding signers' graves during the summer and fall of 2000, I was motivated to keep going, especially if I found myself anywhere nearby to a grave I had not yet visited. Going home to Connecticut for Thanksgiving put me back in New England and provided the opportunity to again meet up with my childhood friend Jonathan, who lived near the University of Connecticut in the eastern part of the state. Jonathan was willing to continue the search with me, even after our trip through New Haven earlier in the year. He had spent most of his youth in Rhode Island and was eager to help me find the two signers from the state: Stephen Hopkins, buried in Providence, and William Ellery, buried in Newport.

I drove out to Jonathan's home and from there we rode to Rhode Island. Considering I grew up in Connecticut, I have few recollections of going to Rhode Island, so I was glad to have him with me to help navigate the Ocean State. We began in Providence, where we fairly easily found our way to the North Burial Ground. It is a pretty neat old cemetery, so it was fun to wander around and see some of the stones. The cemetery dates back to about 1700. Before that time, people tended to bury relatives in family plots on their own property, but as the city grew, a public burying ground was needed. A number of prominent early citizens of Providence were buried at the Old North Burial Ground. Stephen Hopkins, to me, was the most recognizable name on the list.[167]

Hopkins died in 1785 at the age of 78. In an old biography written about him, it stated that he did not suffer the effects of age:

HIS LAST ILLNESS WAS LONG, BUT TO THE PERIOD OF HIS DISSOLUTION, HE RETAINED THE FULL POSSESSION OF HIS FACULTIES. A VAST ASSEMBLAGE OF PERSONS, CONSISTING OF JUDGES OF THE COURTS, THE PRESIDENT, PROFESSORS AND STUDENTS OF THE COLLEGE, TOGETHER WITH THE CITIZENS OF THE TOWN, AND INHABITANTS OF THE STATE, FOLLOWED THE REMAINS OF THIS EMINENT MAN TO HIS RESTING: PLACE IN THE GRAVE.[168]

Fig 63: Stephen Hopkins' grave, North Burial Ground, Providence, Rhode Island

---

167   "North Burial Ground Project," on ric.edu/northburialground/history.html, accessed on March 24, 2019, http://www.ric.edu/northburialground/history.html.

168   Rev. Charles A. Goodrich, *Lives of the Signers to the Declaration of Independence* (New York, NY: William Reed & Co, 1856), 149-153, on colonialhall.com/hopkins/Hopkins, accessed on March 24, 2019, http://colonialhall.com/hopkins/hopkins3.php.

This implies to me, that if all these prominent people followed Hopkins to the cemetery, then he should really be there. Usually the clue that a person has been moved is that the signer died before the cemetery was created. The North Burial Ground opened in 1700, and Hopkins died in 1785. I have not come across any reasons to suspect that Hopkins was moved or not buried under the obelisk that today marks his grave. I would guess the stone over the grave is more recent than 1785. The people of Providence, whenever they placed it there, found a lot to say about their patriotic hero. I especially like the poem found on the north side of the gravestone:

> HERE LIES THE MAN IN FATEFUL HOUR,
> WHO BOLDLY STEMM'D TYRANNIC POW'R.
> AND HELD HIS HAND IN THAT DECREE,
> WHICH BADE AMERICA BE FREE!
> —ARNOLD'S POEMS[169]

When I think of Stephen Hopkins, I can't help but think of how he is portrayed in the musical *1776*, as the old, heavy-drinking curmudgeon who is out in the privy while the vote on independence happened. There are probably some liberties taken with his character, as I have often read that Hopkins was a Quaker who would not have indulged to excess with alcohol. Perhaps the movie script writers discovered John Adams' quote about Stephen Hopkins which said, "His Custom was to drink nothing all day nor till Eight O Clock, in the Evening, and then his Beveredge was Jamaica Spirit and Water. It gave him Wit, Humour, Anecdotes, Science and Learning." Adams then continued, "Hopkins never drank to excess,

---

169 "Stephen Hopkins," on dsdi1776.com/signers-by-state/stephen-hopkins, accessed on March 24, 2019, www.dsdi1776.com/signers-by-state/stephen-hopkins/.

but all he drank was immediately not only converted into Wit, Sense, Knowledge, and good humour, but inspired Us all with similar qualities."[170]

The positive comments from a colleague and the flowery sentiments written on his gravestone attest to Stephen Hopkins' popularity and dedication to the people of Rhode Island. One last interesting note comes from Hopkins himself. In his later years he suffered from an ailment that caused him to shake. As he signed the Declaration of Independence he supposedly said, "My hand trembles, my heart does not."[171] While an actor portraying Hopkins in *1776* receives many laughs, perhaps the image of the trembling elderly signer seems a more proper way to remember this New England patriot.

The grave hunt continued that day in Rhode Island, as we moved on to Newport in search of William Ellery. He does not even make it to the musical *1776*, but one of his actions does. Assuming the writers and producers did not want to include all 56 characters in the musical, stories about Ellery and Hopkins combined to form one Rhode Island representative. In the final scene, as they are about to sign the Declaration, Hancock asks Hopkins to sit down. Hopkins says no, that he wants to remember each man's face as he signs. That quote actually came from Ellery, the other Rhode Island representative. "I was determined to see how they all looked as they signed what might be their death warrant. I placed myself beside the secretary, Charles Thomson, and eyed each closely as he affixed his name to the document. Undaunted resolution was displayed in every countenance."[172]

---

170   John Adams autobiography, part 1, "John Adams," through 1776, sheet 28 of 53 [electronic edition]. Adams Family Papers: An Electronic Archive. Massachusetts Historical Society. http://www.masshist.org/digitaladams/.

171   "Stephen Hopkins," on dsdi1776.com/signers-by-state/stephen-hopkins, accessed on March 24, 2019, www.dsdi1776.com/signers-by-state/stephen-hopkins/.

172   Robert T. Conrad, editor, *Sanderson's Biography of the Signers of the Declaration of Independence* (Philadelphia: Thomas, Cowperthwait and Co., 1847), 209.

Newport has a lot of Revolutionary War history, which I would explore on a later visit, but this trip was all about finding William Ellery. Jonathan and I continued on to the Common Ground Cemetery, Newport's oldest cemetery, created in the 1660s.[173] Ellery lived to 92 years old, one of three signers to reach 90, besides John Adams and Charles Carroll. He died in 1820, apparently still of sound mind, as he was reading books until the end. A 1913 biography described his last day:

ON THE FIFTEENTH OF FEBRUARY, 1820, MR. ELLERY ROSE AS USUAL AT HIS HOME IN NEWPORT AND SEATED HIMSELF IN THE ARMLESS FLAG-BOTTOM CHAIR WHICH HE HAD USED FOR HALF A CENTURY. HE BEGAN TO READ TULLEY'S OFFICES IN THE ORIGINAL, USING NO GLASSES, THOUGH THE PRINT WAS SMALL. TO HIS PHYSICIAN, WHO HAD HAPPENED IN AND FOUND HIM LOOKING THIN AND PALE, HE SAID: "I AM GOING OFF THE STAGE OF LIFE, AND IT IS A GREAT BLESSING THAT I GO FREE FROM SICKNESS, PAIN, AND SORROW." AS HIS WEAKNESS INCREASED, HE WAS ASSISTED BY HIS DAUGHTER TO HIS BED, WHERE HE SAT UPRIGHT AND BEGAN TO READ CICERO DE OFFICIIS. A FEW MOMENTS LATER, WITHOUT A STRUGGLE OR OTHER VISIBLE SIGN, HE PASSED AWAY AS IF ENTERING ON A PEACEFUL SLEEP, HIS POSTURE ERECT AND THE BOOK STILL CLASPED IN HIS HAND.[174]

---

173 "Common Burying Ground and Island Cemetery," on tclf.org/landscapes/common-burying-ground, accessed on March 24, 2019, tclf.org/landscapes/common-burying-ground.

174 Henry Robinson Palmer, *The Rhode Island Signers of the Declaration of Independence* (Providence: Rhode Island Society of the Sons of the American Revolution, 1913), 31.

Ellery was born in Newport and died in Newport, and since the cemetery where he was buried existed years before his death, it seems likely he was buried there. The Society of the Descendants of the Signers claims that the Rhode Island State Society of the Daughters of the American Revolution restored Ellery's gravesite in 1965.[175]

This restoration may explain one of the more frustrating elements of the grave search—the closed gate. Luckily, this situation was not as bad as others I encountered on the quest. Ellery's plot was enclosed by a gate, which made it difficult to snap a photograph.

I was at least able to see through it, as opposed to George Clymer's, where I originally couldn't even access the stone for a photo. Jonathan, at this point, was pretty invested in the search. This was now the fourth grave he had been to with me and having come this far he was not satisfied with the photograph having bars in the picture. He took one for the team and climbed over the fence so that I could have a clear picture of Ellery's grave. I appreciate his dedication to the cause, since I was not going to get over that fence myself. I am lucky to have had so many friends help me along the way to complete this project. Our Rhode Island trip was a great success and inspired me to continue on the quest for more signers' graves.

Fig 64: Fence around William Ellery's grave, Common Ground Cemetery, Newport, Rhode Island

175 "William Ellery," on dsdi1776.com/signers-by-state/william-ellery, accessed on April 5, 2019, www.dsdi1776.com/signers-by-state/william-ellery/.

Fig 65 and 66: Photos of William Ellery's grave, Common Ground Cemetery, Newport, Rhode Island (photo by Jonathan Chesler)

XVIII

New Hampshire

Findagrave.com was my best friend as I searched for the signers' graves. The website, along with the fact that I lived on the East Coast, eased the process of finding and photographing the graves. The travel sometimes proved challenging, but I was lucky to have supportive friends and family willing to play along. In some cases, it would surprise me how eager people were to help.

One Thanksgiving, I was home for the holiday with the family in Connecticut. My father's birthday falls around Thanksgiving and we were going to spend a father-daughter day together. We had a few options for the day's activity. I was hoping for a road trip to Boston to watch a hockey game. Dad surprised me with his choice. He preferred to go graving in New Hampshire. It was his birthday, so he got to make the final decision. In the end, I'm glad he did. I had yet to visit any of the three signers in New Hampshire. With our route plotted out we were pretty confident we could do all three in one day, even with limited daylight in November.

We began our adventure in Portsmouth, New Hampshire, a coastal town with plenty of history. I had been there before, but never focused much on the historic sites. On this day it was strictly about the cemetery. The signer in question was William Whipple, a prominent figure in colonial New Hampshire. He had been active in the state government and the military, participating in the Battle of Saratoga. Later in life, he served as a judge. At the end he suffered from a painful illness and in what seems unusual for the times, he asked that an autopsy be done after his death. He wanted people to learn from his pain. A relative performed the autopsy and determined his death was related to hardening of the arteries around the heart.[176] Whipple seemed prepared for death, as a quotation from an obituary posted on a family website said, "He viewed his approaching dissolution with a heroic fortitude, in full confidence that He who made him knew best how to dispose of him."[177] When he died in 1785 he was buried in the Old North Cemetery in Portsmouth.

Dad and I had a fairly easy time finding the cemetery, the second oldest in the city dating back to 1753. I have encountered many cemeteries over the course of this search, but I don't recall one as disappointing as this one. Tombstones were broken. Trash littered the ground. I remember taking a photo of my dad, trying to put pieces of a headstone back together. There is great potential though, with a nice view of the North Mill Pond, yet such a sad situation for all those resting at Old North Cemetery.

---

176   Dorothy Mansfield Vaughan, "This Was a Man: A Biography of General William Whipple," read by author on February 26, 1964, accessed on April 6, 2019, https://whipple.org/william/thiswasaman.html.

177   "William Whipple," on dsdi1776.com/signers-by-state/william-whipple, accessed on April 6, 2019, www.dsdi1776.com/signers-by-state/william-whipple/.

Fig 67: Dad with broken headstone, Old North
Cemetery, Portsmouth, New Hampshire

It has been many years since I visited and I'm encouraged to see websites that refer to Portsmouth cleaning up and restoring its historic cemeteries. Apparently it has long been a place to party and drink, walk dogs, and sleep if homeless. I am hopeful that the community will work to improve the surroundings at Old North Cemetery and preserve its history for the future. Besides Whipple, John Langdon, a signer of the Constitution, also rests in this cemetery.[178]

178 "Portsmouth's Historic Cemeteries," on cityofportsmouth.com/publicworks/grounds/ portsmouths-historic-cemeteries, accessed on April 6, 2019, www.cityofportsmouth. com/publicworks/grounds/portsmouths-historic-cemeteries.

Fig 68 and 69: William Whipple's grave, Old North Cemetery, Portsmouth, New Hampshire

Whipple's resting place is in the middle of the yard marked with a flagpole. It looks like an above-ground tomb with a wordy epitaph carved on a slab on top, highlighting his career. This slab was placed in 1976 in honor of the bicentennial,[179] so I wonder what might have been there before. The stone could have deteriorated over time. I'm glad that the county took an interest to fix his tomb and allow visitors to know more about his contributions.

Beyond the conditions of the cemetery, there is another interesting story to be found. Nearby to William Whipple's grave is the grave of Prince Whipple. Not the son of the signer, but the slave of the signer. One of my historian friends, Ernie, has been fascinated since I started this search about the number of signers of the Declaration of Independence who owned slaves. As someone who talks about Thomas Jefferson frequently too, I am often confronted with the irony of the subject. Here was this group of men, risking their lives and fighting for this cause of

179 "William Whipple—Portsmouth, N.H." on waymarking.com/waymarks/WME6K0_ William_Whipple_Portsmouth_NH, accessed on April 6, 2019, http://www. waymarking.com/waymarks/WME6K0_William_Whipple_Portsmouth_NH.

independence from England, when many denied that independence to others. I promised Ernie I would further explore this and find out how many of the signers actually owned slaves. Most did.

William Whipple faced this dilemma as well. While serving in the Revolutionary War, Prince, his slave, traveled with him. A story told in *Rambles About Portsmouth* from 1859 described Gen. Whipple and Prince preparing to move out for the Battle of Saratoga. The general gave orders for Prince to get the horses ready to leave while he attended a meeting. Upon returning, Prince had not done what he'd been told. When Gen. Whipple questioned Prince and his moodiness, Prince replied, "You are going to fight for your liberty, but I have none to fight for." Supposedly Whipple responded, "Prince, behave like a man, and do your duty, and from this hour, you shall be free."[180] It probably took a little more than that, as Prince Whipple had to petition for his freedom years later. He would end up marrying and living in a house on the Whipples' property, outliving Gen. Whipple by twelve years. When he died in 1797, he was also buried in the Old North Cemetery. His grave was finally marked with a headstone in July 1908, by the Storer Post, Grand Army of the Republic of Portsmouth, New Hampshire.[181]

In researching Prince Whipple, I was struck by the *Rambles About Portsmouth's* authors' assessment of Whipple and slavery. Written in 1859, just before the Civil War, they wrote about William Whipple as a young man working in the shipping industry, sailing around the world, including a voyage to Africa. "The blemish of that dark living freight which his vessel brought away, has not been wholly obliterated

---

180 Joseph Foster, "Prince Whipple of Portsmouth: A Colored Veteran of the American Revolution," *The Granite Monthly: A New Hampshire Magazine*, Vol. XL, No.8 (Aug 1908): 287.

181 Foster, "Prince Whipple of Portsmouth: A Colored Veteran of the American Revolution," 287.

by the fame which shines around his name on the immortal scroll of our country's glory."[182] I like the words chosen here, as well as the meaning, since it addresses the sticky issue of Declaration signers owning slaves—a subject still hard to explain centuries later.

Next, we were on to Kingston, New Hampshire, in search of Josiah Bartlett. His name may sound familiar to fans of the television show, *The West Wing*, as the presidential character. In real life he was probably the second person to sign the Declaration after John Hancock's sprawling signature, as delegates voted and signed by colony- starting in the north.[183] Bartlett had an illustrious career as a doctor and politician. He died in 1795 and was buried in Kingston's Plains Cemetery—which had been established in 1725.[184] Dad and I did well in finding the cemetery and enjoyed walking around looking for Bartlett's grave. Like Whipple's, it was an above-ground tomb with a relatively new-looking slab on top. I can't find any confirmation, but the engraving on both Whipple's and Bartlett's tombs look similar. Maybe Bartlett also received a bicentennial update.

Fig 70 and 71: Josiah Bartlett's grave, Plains Cemetery, Kingston,
New Hampshire

---

182   Charles W. Brewster, *Rambles about Portsmouth* (Portsmouth, N.H.: Lewis W. Brewster, 1873), 152.

183   Ferris, *Signers of the Declaration*, 39.

184   Bob Pothier, Jr. and Ellen Lavoie, *History of Kingston, New Hampshire, 1694-1994* (Kingston, NH: Kingston's 300th Anniversary Committee, 1994), IV-6.

The final stop for this successful graving day was Merrimack, New Hampshire, in search of Matthew Thornton. As we drove down the road we saw a monument that we assumed was Thornton's grave. This was actually a monument built to honor Thornton years later in 1892, located right next to the small cemetery where he was buried. He died in Massachusetts while visiting his daughter in 1803. His grave is marked by a simple stone and local folks felt his historic contributions should be marked more significantly.

Fig 72 and 73: Matthew Thornton grave, Merrimack, New Hampshire

Thornton was born in Ireland, coming to America as a small child. He lived in a few New England towns before settling in the Merrimack area. He practiced medicine and was elected president of the first state provincial Congress. He was sent to the Continental Congress after the Declaration debate, vote, and signing, arriving in November 1776. He asked if he could still sign the document after most had already done so.[185] John Adams wrote, "We have from New Hampshire a Colonel Thornton, a physician by profession, a man of humor. He has a large budget of droll stories with which he entertains company perpetually." [186]

When the Declaration was signed on August 2, delegates signed by colony, so all those from one colony appear together on the paper. Looking at the signed copy of the Declaration, the New Hampshire delegates Bartlett and Whipple signed at the top of the far right column, followed by the Massachusetts, Rhode Island, and Connecticut signers. Thornton's name is at the bottom of that column. At the time Thornton signed, the war's outcome was still in question. This was a risky thing to do and one he consciously chose, asking to put his name to the revolutionary document.

Thornton died in 1803 at age 89. At the 1892 monument dedication, W.W. Bailey spoke of the importance of remembering this signer:

> SUCH MEMORIALS SERVE A USEFUL PURPOSE. THEY HONOR THE DEAD AND STIMULATE THE PATRIOTISM OF THE LIVING. THEY ARE EVIDENCES OF APPRECIATION OF BRAVE AND PATRIOTIC SERVICES BY A GRATEFUL PEOPLE. FEW PERSONS NOW LIVING HAVE LOOKED UPON THE FACE OF A REVOLUTIONARY PATRIOT. THEY HAVE ALL LONG SINCE PASSED AWAY. OUR KNOWLEDGE AND IMPRESSIONS OF

---

185   Ferris, *Signers of the Declaration*, 139-140.
186   Bakeless, *Signers of the Declaration*, 230.

THEM AND OF THEIR DEEDS ARE FROM HISTORY. THERE
MAY BE DANGER THAT LAPSE OF TIME AND SUBSEQUENT
IMPORTANT EVENTS IN THE HISTORY OF OUR NATION MAY
TEND TO OBSCURE THE GLORY OF THEIR ACHIEVEMENTS,
AND TO DIMINISH THAT DUE SENSE OF GRATITUDE THAT
OUGHT TO EXIST IN THE HEARTS OF ALL SUCCEEDING
GENERATIONS AS LONG AS OUR NATION SHALL ENDURE.
MONUMENTS AND STATUES ILLUSTRATE, EMPHASIZE, AND
KEEP IN REMEMBRANCE GREAT FACTS AND CHARACTERS
IN HISTORY. THIS MONUMENT WILL REMIND COMING
GENERATIONS OF THE LIFE, CHARACTER, AND PUBLIC
SERVICE OF MATTHEW THORNTON.[187]

Bailey summed up in 1892 exactly how I feel today about the signers' graves. Time is even further removed from the events of 1776. The
memory of these men and their sacrifices are fading away. Without monuments, gravestones, diaries, and letters, these patriots may be forgotten.
Some are little known beyond their own communities. I wonder how
many people drive by Thornton's monument and do not realize why it
is there or what role he played in history. That is why I have found it so
surprising that some signers were treated so poorly in death. The final
resting place should at least be the one spot where they could be honored
and remembered, yet in some cases, that final resting place is unknown or
not maintained. A group has recognized this situation too. The Society
of the Descendants of the Signers of the Declaration of Independence

---

187 State of New Hampshire, *Addresses at the Dedication of the Monument Erected to the
      Memory of Matthew Thornton at Merrimack, N.H., September 29, 1892* (Concord, N.H.:
      The Republican Press Association, 1894), 27.

began putting markers at signers' graves in 2004 to honor their service.[188] Let's hope this will help future generations remember the efforts of those in the early days of the nation.

I really appreciate the interest my dad took in this project. I look back fondly to that day we spent together traipsing through New Hampshire and am glad he chose to spend his birthday on the search for the signers.

Fig 74: Matthew Thornton Monument, Merrimack, New Hampshire

---

188   "Signers grave recognition," on dsdi1776.com/signers-grave-recognition, accessed on April 6, 2019, www.dsdi1776.com/signers-grave-recognition/.

XIX

North Carolina

y friend Bert had a job working for the National Park Service at Kings Mountain National Military Park in South Carolina. He had been there for over a year when Michael and I decided to study up on our Revolutionary War history, especially the Southern Campaign, and go visit. Of course, never with just one goal in mind, this presented an opportunity for me to visit some new national parks, get some passport stamps, and find some more Declaration signers' graves. We had made plans to visit Bert before this, but various scheduling conflicts arose. So we decided to make our own plans, chose a convenient time, what sites we wanted to see, and then consulted Bert. As it turned out, Bert was on special assignment that weekend and wouldn't be in town when we planned to visit. The trip was scheduled, the sites were calling, and I was anxious to continue my grave quest.

Strategically, this was going to be an easy time for graving. One weekend would lead to four graves seen in two states. In a way, Georgia and North Carolina had made it easy for me. They must have known someone would do a project like this someday. Both states decided to consolidate their patriots into one, easy-to-visit stop.

In the case of North Carolina, the destination was Guilford Courthouse National Military Park in Greensboro. This was our first stop as we headed south from the Washington, DC area. Traveling south in February, one wouldn't expect weather problems, but on this particular day the storm was hitting from the south. I have the habit of falling asleep in a car if I'm not driving, so Michael maneuvered the car through the snow as I slept, made more difficult by Southern drivers not used to snow. We finally arrived at Guilford Courthouse, site of a 1781 Revolutionary War battle, to find the park quiet and covered with snow and ice. After talking to the park ranger we realized we had just missed our friend Bert by minutes, as he had stopped in hoping to catch up with us. This was before everyone owned a cellphone and coordinating a visit was simple.

The snow impacted our visit. With many of the tour roads closed, we embarked on foot to see the park. Of critical importance to me was the monument adjacent to the large equestrian statue of Nathanael Greene. The smaller memorial paid tribute to two of North Carolina's three signers of the Declaration of Independence, William Hooper and John Penn.

Having traipsed around in the cold for some time, it was just as we arrived at the Hooper-Penn Monument that my faithful camera started acting up. It must have just been temperamental to the cold because after making all sorts of funny noises, not counting my whines and groans at its dysfunction, I was able to photograph the monument that serves as a grave for these two signers. Of particular interest to me was the quote on the stone from John Adams describing his friend Hooper. Who would expect a quote from a Massachusetts man on a stone in North Carolina? "Lee, Henry, and Hooper were the orators of the Congress," 1774.[189]

This does not mark the original burial sites for William Hooper and John Penn. In a flurry of patriotism, North Carolina decided to make Guilford Courthouse a shrine to honor the state's founding fathers and early history. Though there was no connection between these men and the battle fought in 1781, remains were moved from original burial spots to this site in 1894. The plan was for the third North Carolina signer to also be included here, Joseph Hewes. However, Hewes died in Philadelphia in 1779 and was buried in the Christ Church

Fig 75: Hooper-Penn Monument and grave, Guilford Courthouse National Military Park, Greensboro, North Carolina

Burial Ground. When those creating the new memorial wanted to bring Hewes' remains to Greensboro, they were told that Hewes' original burial spot was unmarked.[190] Hewes was left in Philadelphia, where today a stone sits for him. (See Chapter 13.)

The fascination with these men and their graves does not just stop at the actual burial sites. The obsession, for some unknown reason, goes deeper. Knowing that these men have been moved from one site to

---

189   Baker, *The Monuments at Guilford Courthouse National Military Park*, 47.

190   Baker, *The Monuments at Guilford Courthouse National Military Park*, 46.

another means there is more to the story. In some cases, it means going to the original gravesite, which I have done for both of these men.

William Hooper died in Hillsborough, North Carolina. I was there once with Bert, having met him in Raleigh to do some history and probably take in some hockey. We had gone to Bennett Place in Durham to see where Johnston's army had surrendered at the end of the Civil War. Bert knew the town of Hillsborough to be historic and thought I would enjoy it, especially with a signer connection. We made our way to the old cemetery and found the stone for William Hooper.

I had visited Hillsborough long before I began digging deeper (a very bad choice of words in this situation) into the signers' grave stories. I did not think to ask enough questions while there regarding the reburial of William Hooper in Greensboro. I think back to Edenton where I learned in detail about the ceremony in which James Wilson was dug up and transferred back to Philadelphia. Until I have the chance to return, I contacted the historical society in Hillsborough to inquire more about Hooper's reburial and searched North Carolina history websites. A Hooper biography on the NCpedia site mentioned the process:

Fig 76: William Hooper's original grave, Old Town Cemetery, Hillsborough, North Carolina

"On 25 Apr. 1894, the grave was opened at dawn before various family representatives, and a very few discernible relics—part of a button and a nail or two—were placed in an envelope and removed, together with the covering sandstone slab, to the Guilford Courthouse National Military Park, Greensboro."[191]

I know of many signers who have been reburied and often wondered what remains moved from one gravesite to another. This description provides unusual detail and fits with what I remember from the visit to Hillsborough—that some of Hooper's remains moved to Greensboro and some stayed behind. This seems not only morbid, but sad when considering the sacrifice these men made for the creation of the nation. I think back to Connecticut's Roger Sherman on the Green in New Haven, with a nice headstone in the Grove Street Cemetery that people assume he rests under. Some of these men suffered unbelievable fates in death. Someone like Hooper is probably hardly remembered outside his home state today, yet during his lifetime he risked a lot by signing the Declaration.

The article then mentions that Hooper's original sandstone slab was returned to Hillsborough and the monument in Greensboro built. One would think that was the end of Hooper's story, but there is a little more. While both Hooper and Penn were reburied in Greensboro in 1894, they were not done moving yet. In 1976, they came to their present location from another spot on the battlefield. Supposedly the original battlefield burial site caused trouble for drivers on the park road.[192] Guilford Courthouse National Military Park has a photograph on its website of the North Carolina Signers' Monument dating back to about 1895 with

---

191 "Hooper, William," on ncpedia.org/biography/hooper-william, accessed on April 6, 2019, www.ncpedia.org/biography/hooper-william.

192 "Hooper Penn Monument," on ncpedia.org/monument/hooper-penn-monument, accessed on April 7, 2019, www.ncpedia.org/monument/hooper-penn-monument.

a caption that says the monument is in its original location.[193] After two moves, let's hope these men can finally rest in peace.

On another Southern adventure, my friend Michael and I searched for the original burial site of John Penn, the other North Carolina signer buried under the monument in Greensboro. We had plotted out a long weekend to tour historic sites on the eastern side of North Carolina, pretty focused on research about the signers. It was this trip that we visited Edenton, North Carolina, and learned about James Wilson. We also visited the plantation that was home to South Carolina signer Thomas Lynch, Jr. We hoped to meet up with our friend Bert, who was working in South Carolina at the time. He must have shared with me information regarding John Penn's burial place in Stovall, North Carolina, which is in Granville County near the Virginia state line.

A series of books by Daniel Barefoot really came in handy. In *Touring Revolutionary War Sites in North Carolina*, the author gives specific directions for finding the site of Penn's property and original gravesite.[194] In one of the more unusual experiences on this hunt, we drove down back roads and eventually a dirt road that ended in a circular drive in the woods. Awaiting us was a hand-made sign announcing our arrival at the John Penn home site. The area was well marked, with the letter stickers one finds at a hardware store on wooden posts. We saw no other people while we were out there, but really appreciated the work that had gone into preserving and marking this historic spot.

---

193   "The Guilford Battle Ground Company," on nps.gov/parkhistory/online_books/hh/30/hh30q.htm, accessed on April 7, 2019, www.nps.gov/parkhistory/online_books/hh/30/hh30q.htm.

194   Daniel W. Barefoot, *Touring North Carolina's Revolutionary War Sites* (Winston-Salem, NC: John F. Blair Publisher, 1998), 429.

Fig 77 and 78: John Penn's original grave site, Stovall,
North Carolina

An article appeared in the Spartanburg, South Carolina *Herald-Journal* in 1998, highlighting the work that the local Daughters of the American Revolution (DAR) chapter was doing to preserve the John Penn site. Penn lived here, died in 1787 at the age of 46, and was buried here until 1894 when he and Hooper were reburied in Greensboro at the Guilford Courthouse battlefield. As with Hooper's story though, some questions exist, especially since Penn's remains would have been moved over 100 years after his death. The reporter spoke to William Dartt, a volunteer who helped to preserve the Penn site.

> DARTT SAID HE UNDERSTANDS THE GOVERNMENT ONLY TOOK A PORTION OF THE REMAINS FROM THE GRAVE, THAT THERE IS ONLY A SMALL BOX AT THE GUILFORD PARK. AND THAT IN ALL LIKELIHOOD MOST OF THE REMAINS ARE STILL RIGHT HERE, IN THE GROUND, ON THIS SITE.[195]

This sounds very familiar after the Hooper in Hillsborough situation. Both of these signers were disturbed years after their deaths to be "moved" to another location. In both instances it seems as if most of their remains remained in the original grave. What a strange situation for these founding fathers. What did the move actually accomplish? More visitors come in contact with the North Carolina signers at Guilford Courthouse than people visiting the woods in Stovall. But in many cases, like Penn, the signer's remains were moved while the wife's remains were left behind. It is a sad ending for these patriots, moved around and separated from their families.

The site in Stovall was so unusual. We followed the handmade signs through the woods and found the family graveyard. A fence surrounded the graves of Penn and his family. Another particularly interesting aspect of the site was the existence of the Penns' slave cemetery. As mentioned previously, the idea of these Declaration signers fighting for their independence while owning others is hard to reconcile today. Even well-established historic sites, like Mount Vernon and Monticello, have reconsidered their interpretation of slavery. Yet in the middle of the

---

195   Charlie Richards, "DAR Honors Grave Site of N.C. Patriot John Penn," *Spartanburg Herald-Journal*, August 9, 1998, B5.

woods in North Carolina, not only is the Penn family cemetery labeled and preserved, but also the graveyard of the Penns' slaves. It is certainly nice to see folks who have taken an interest in the local history enough to identify and preserve a place that could easily have been forgotten.

Fig 79: John Penn's original grave site, Stovall, North Carolina

Fig 80: Sign at Penn's original gravesite, Stovall, North Carolina

The more I have researched the North Carolina signers the sadder I have become as I think about why and how they were moved. I can appreciate the efforts of Judge David Schenck, who worked hard to preserve the Guilford Courthouse battlefield. Did moving Hooper and Penn add to the significance of the site? They really had no connection to the battle, and a monument to them could have been built to recognize their efforts on behalf of independence, without moving them from their respective burial sites. Speaking of moving them, it appears that little of the signers' remains were moved to Greensboro, which makes for an even sadder story. Why weren't these men left to rest in peace, alongside family members? It all adds to the strange treatment these men received after "pledging their lives, their fortunes, and their sacred honor."

I joked at the beginning of this chapter about how much I appreciated having a one-stop shop for signers at a place like Guilford Courthouse. While it made the grave hunt simpler, the real story saddens me and makes me wonder why so many of these signers were not left where they were originally buried. No one should suffer these indignities, especially those who risked everything for their country.

XX

Georgia

On the same trip that Michael and I visited Greensboro and the North Carolina signers, we also went to Augusta, Georgia, to find the majority of the Georgia signers. Like North Carolina, Georgia tried to put all three signers together in one location. Again, like North Carolina, Georgia would only be two for three.

None of the Georgia signers were originally from Georgia. George Walton was born in Virginia,[196] Lyman Hall was born in Connecticut,[197] and Button Gwinnett was born in England.[198] Yet they would all represent Georgia at the Continental Congress and sign the Declaration in August 1776.

---

196 Ferris, *Signers of the Declaration*, 141.

197 Ferris, *Signers of the Declaration*, 65.

198 Ferris, *Signers of the Declaration*, 62.

There are similarities between the North Carolina and Georgia sign-ers' stories. In each state, someone years later thought the state's signers should be reburied together. Each state had three signers, yet when they tried to rebury them together, only two could be found. In Georgia's case, the missing signer was Button Gwinnett, who had died after a duel with Lachlan McIntosh in 1777. At the time the other signers were moved to Augusta, no one knew where Gwinnett's remains were located. While he now has a stone in the Colonial Park Cemetery in Savannah, there is debate whether his remains are under that stone.

We were really struck on the visit to Augusta by another set of similar-ities. The Signers' Monument in Augusta had much in common with the Washington Monument on the National Mall in Washington, DC. Both are obelisks. While Washington's is 555 feet, 5 and 1/8 inches, Augusta's is fifty feet tall. July 4, 1848 was a significant date for each structure—Washington's Monument had its cornerstone laid, while Augusta's Signers' Monument was dedicated on that day. Similar groups were involved in both monuments. At the dedication in Augusta, participants included Freema-sons, Odd Fellows, and Sons of Temperance.[199] Walk down the steps of the Washington Monument and find stones to each of those groups, who wanted to honor George Washington by contributing to his monument. It is interesting to find these historical connections.

An article written in 1886 by Charles C. Jones, Jr. described how Georgia's signers ended up in Augusta:

IT WAS THE INTENTION OF THE PUBLIC SPIRITED CITIZENS
WHO BUILDED IT TO COMMIT TO FINAL REPOSE BENEATH
THE FOUNDATION STONES OF THIS MONUMENT THE

---

199   Charles C. Jones, Jr., "Monument to Gwinnett, Hall, and Walton," *The Magazine of American History with Notes and Queries*, Vol XVII (Jan-Jun 1887), 134.

REMAINS OF THE DISTINGUISHED PATRIOTS WHOSE JOINT MEMORIES IT WAS DESIGNED TO PERPETUATE. WITH THIS END IN VIEW A COMMITTEE WAS APPOINTED TO OPEN THE GRAVES AND SUPERINTEND THE REMOVAL AND THE REINHUMATION OF THE BONES OF THESE WORTHIES.[200]

Obviously Gwinnett's remains were not found for the move in 1848. The article explained that Lyman Hall's remains were easily found, as Hall's original grave was marked on his plantation, Shell Bluff in Burke County, where he had died in 1790.[201] After reading of so many remains being moved, but probably not really moved, I wonder where Hall really rests. Jones' article says, "All that remained of his honored dust was capable of easy identification."[202] It is hard to imagine what that means when he

Fig 81: Signers' Monument, Augusta, Georgia

was reburied nearly sixty years after his death.

Once Hall's remains were moved to Augusta, his original headstone marked an empty grave. To honor his Connecticut origins, the headstone was sent to his hometown of Wallingford. An elaborate ceremony was

200 Jones, "Monument to Gwinnett, Hall, and Walton," 133.
201 Jones, "Monument to Gwinnett, Hall, and Walton," 133.
202 Jones, "Monument to Gwinnett, Hall, and Walton," 133.

held as the headstone was placed in the Center Street Cemetery on July 5, 1858. A journal article from 1903 describes the all-day event, including the marble tablet's procession from the depot to the cemetery accompanied by military and musical tributes, a reading of the Declaration of Independence, speeches, toasts, and fireworks. Of thirteen toasts, the fourth was in honor of Lyman Hall: "The friend of human rights, the advocate of freedom, a signer of the immortal Declaration. His fame is embalmed in the hearts of the people who commemorate this occasion by placing his tombstone among the graves of his ancestors."[203]

While I have yet to look for the location of Hall's original grave in Georgia, I did visit the original headstone in Wallingford. My dad and I got up early one morning and took a ride to the Center Street Cemetery. We walked around the cemetery and found the stone. It seemed a little strange to make a trip to a cemetery solely to see the stone, knowing there were no remains under it, but considering what happened to some of these signers after they died, visiting a headstone does not seem all that unusual.

Fig 82: Lyman Hall's original gravestone, Center Street Cemetery, Wallingford, Connecticut

203 Harry O. Hall, "Dr. Lyman Hall, One of the Signers of the Declaration of Independence," *The American Monthly Magazine*, Vol XXII, No. 4 (April 1903), 340.

Harry Hall ended his 1903 article about his ancestor Lyman Hall with these statements:

THUS DID TWO GREAT STATES IN THE UNION IN THE FORMATION OF WHICH HE BORE SO CONSPICUOUS A PART, VIE WITH EACH OTHER IN DOING HONOR TO THE MEMORY OF LYMAN HALL, THE PATRIOT AND CHAMPION OF LIBERTY. WELL MAY WE, WHO ARE LIVING IN THE FULL ENJOYMENT OF THE BLESSINGS CONFERRED UPON US BY THE LIVES AND SERVICES OF SUCH NOBLE MEN, BOW IN REVERENCE AT THE MENTION OF THEIR NAMES, AND AGAIN RENEW OUR VOWS TO REMAIN LOYAL TO THE PRINCIPLES WHICH THEY ADVOCATED, TO REVERE THEIR MEMORIES, AND TO SACRIFICE EVEN OUR LIVES IN UPHOLDING AND PERPETUATING THE INSTITUTIONS WHICH THEY FOUNDED.[204]

I like what Hall said here and wish that more people today kept these thoughts in mind. Most people would not recognize many of the signers' names. Considering what happened to some of the signers in life and after death, these sentiments have been forgotten by many over time. No one should suffer the fate of these men, having remains moved and separated, especially those who risked all for their country.

George Walton was the other Georgia signer who was moved to the Augusta monument from his family cemetery at Rosney, about nine miles from Augusta. He died in 1804. The article from 1886 explained that while finding Gwinnett was impossible and finding Hall was easy, finding Walton's remains was a challenge. Apparently when the move

---

204 Harry O. Hall, "Dr. Lyman Hall, One of the Signers of the Declaration of Independence," *The American Monthly Magazine*, Vol XXII, No. 4 (April 1903), 340.

happened in 1848 there were some elderly folks who remembered the approximate location of Walton's grave, even though it was unmarked. The remains found were confirmed to be those of George Walton, based on the right femur which had evidence of a wound, like that suffered by Walton in December 1778. He was acting as the state's colonial militia commander when the British launched an attack on Savannah. He was hit in the leg, captured, and held as a prisoner.[205]

Walton and Hall were moved to Augusta and rest under the monument at Greene and Monument streets. After learning of other signers' stories, I can't help but wonder whether the remains were really moved to the Augusta monument or were left behind in the original locations. While I admire the state's interest in honoring its founding fathers, in this case, as in North Carolina's situation, it may have been more appropriate to leave the men where they were buried, building a monument to remember them. Like the Lincoln Memorial in Washington, DC, a monument can be built to honor a historical figure without that person being buried underneath. But all of these twists and turns adds to the collection of unusual stories related to the signers and their burial sites.

---

205 Jones, "Monument to Gwinnett, Hall, and Walton," 133.

XXI

New Jersey and New York

By this point, I could look at the list and see that I was getting close to finishing the quest of finding all the signers' graves. I tried to coordinate my travels so that I could find those remaining. Luckily, my friends were willing to help out too. The annual trip with my friends in the summer of 2001 was to see the historic sites of New York state. We weren't going to New York City, but upstate to see a variety of Revolutionary War sites, national parks, minor league baseball stadiums, and whatever else we found along the way. We are usually pretty good about compromising on what we want to visit so that each of us is fairly happy with the stops we make. Thankfully, the boys have humored me a lot along the way as part of this search for the signers.

Heading north from our respective locations in Virginia and South Carolina, Michael, Bert, and I began our trip with a grave stop. We were in search of Abraham Clark, who was buried in Rahway, New Jersey.

Every time I head north through New Jersey, I see the sign for Clark and Rahway and wonder if the town is named for signer Abraham Clark or some member of his family. Apparently the town is named for the signer. This was a relatively easy stop. Not too far off the highway we found the Rahway Cemetery and the grave of Abraham Clark and his wife, Sarah. Clark died in 1794, supposedly after suffering from sunstroke.[206]

Fig 83: Abraham Clark's grave, Rahway   Fig 84: Abraham Clark Monument,
Cemetery, Rahway, New Jersey   Rahway Cemetery, Rahway, New Jersey

Clark's headstone is unique, in that the stones for both Clark and his wife have been preserved within a larger stone, done in 1924 by the local chapter of the Daughters of the American Revolution. As we continued wandering through the cemetery, we came across another monument with Clark's name on it: an obelisk, ten feet tall, built in Clark's honor and dedicated on July 4, 1848, a very busy day in memorialization. The

206 "Abraham Clark," on dsdi1776.com/signers-by-state/abraham-clark, accessed on April 20, 2019, www.dsdi1776.com/signers-by-state/abraham-clark/.

Washington Monument had its cornerstone laid while the Signers'
Monument in Augusta was also dedicated that day. We wondered as
we saw this more recent monument if possibly Clark's remains had been
moved to this site. I contacted the local historical society in Rahway
and received an email response that Clark remains buried under the
older stone. The obelisk was a memorial built by the people of Rahway
to honor him and his work.[207]

Though Clark is not one of the more famous Declaration signers, it
is nice to see him remembered by his community. His obituary in the
New-Jersey Journal of September 17, 1794, described his character:

> ON MONDAY LAST, VERY SUDDENLY, THE HON. ABRAHAM
> CLARK, ESQ. MEMBER FROM THIS STATE, TO THE
> CONGRESS OF THE UNITED STATES, IN THE 69TH YEAR OF
> HIS AGE. IN THE DEATH OF MR. CLARK, HIS FAMILY HAS
> SUSTAINED AN IRRETRIEVABLE LOSS, AND THE STATE IS
> DEPRIVED OF A USEFUL CITIZEN, WHO, FOR FORTY YEARS
> PAST, HAS BEEN EMPLOYED IN THE MOST HONORABLE AND
> CONFIDENTIAL TRUSTS, WHICH HE EVER DISCHARGED WITH
> THAT DISINTERESTEDNESS, ABILITY, AND INDEFATIGABLE
> INDUSTRY…MR. CLARK WAS A MAN OF SOUND JUDGMENT,
> LIVELY WIT, AND VERY SATIRICAL; IN THE EXERCISE OF
> WHICH HE MADE SOMETIMES ENEMIES. AS A CHRISTIAN,
> HE WAS UNIFORM AND CONSISTENT, ADORNING THAT
> RELIGION, THAT HE HAD EARLY MADE A PROFESSION OF,
> BY ACTS OF CHARITY AND BENEVOLENCE.[208]

---

207 "Abraham Clark," on dsdi1776.com/signers-by-state/abraham-clark, accessed on April
20, 2019, www.dsdi1776.com/signers-by-state/abraham-clark/.

208 "Abraham Clark," on dsdi1776.com/signers-by-state/abraham-clark, accessed on April
20, 2019, www.dsdi1776.com/signers-by-state/abraham-clark/.

The vacation continued north as we visited the Roosevelt homes in Hyde Park, the Saratoga battlefield, and Fort Stanwix. We headed west to go to Rochester, Buffalo, and Niagara Falls. Along the way we made a stop in Westernville, New York, to look for the grave of William Floyd.

Floyd was a New York signer from Long Island. He not only served in the Continental Congress, but also led a regiment in the New York militia. During the war his family suffered greatly. They fled to Connecticut for many years, his wife dying there, never returning to their home that was damaged by the British. Eventually he left the Long Island property to his son and moved to Westernville, New York, about forty minutes east of Syracuse. He built a house there very similar to the house he left behind on Long Island.[209] He died in 1821 at age 86 and was buried in the Westernville Presbyterian Church Cemetery.[210]

Fig 85: William Floyd's grave, Westernville Presbyterian Church
Cemetery, Westernville, New York

209   "William Floyd," on dsdi1776.com/members-only/william-floyd, accessed on April 21, 2019, dsdi1776.com/members-only/william-floyd.

210   "The General William Floyd House," on generalwilliamfloydhouse.org/feature.html, accessed on April 21, 2019, www.generalwilliamfloydhouse.org/feature.html.

John Jay, Floyd's colleague, described Floyd's time at the Continental Congress:

COLONEL FLOYD'S CONDUCT WHILE HERE GAINED HIM MUCH
RESPECT. HE MOVED ON STEADY UNIFORM PRINCIPLES,
AND APPEARED ALWAYS TO JUDGE FOR HIMSELF, WHICH,
IN MY OPINION, IS ONE VERY ESSENTIAL QUALIFICATION IN
A DELEGATE, AND ABSOLUTELY NECESSARY TO PREVENT HIS
BEING A MERE TOOL OF FACTIONS.[211]

We had a pretty easy time finding this grave. Westernville is a small town and even without smartphones we could find the church and the cemetery behind it. The guys and I always enjoy wandering around old cemeteries, so we walked around looking at some of the stones. I took a number of photos of Floyd's grave. At the time I do not remember questioning whether Floyd was really buried there. I should have paid more attention to the headstone. According to the website for the Gen. William Floyd House in Westernville, the current headstone was placed there by descendants after the original headstone was sent to the family home on Long Island. The original stone may have deteriorated and the family wanted a grander stone placed over the remains of Floyd and his second wife, Johanna.[212]

Today, the Floyd property in Mastic, New York, is maintained by the National Park Service. Michael, my parents, and I visited the estate on Long Island a few years ago, partly to see the site and partly to confirm where Floyd was buried. The ranger assured me that the burial site in

---

211 Scudiere, *New York's Signers of the Declaration of Independence*, 23.
212 "The General William Floyd House," on generalwilliamfloydhouse.org/feature.html, accessed on April 21, 2019, www.generalwilliamfloydhouse.org/feature.html.

Westernville is Floyd's final resting place. What I didn't realize then
was the headstone situation. I guess I knew there was a family graveyard on the estate in Mastic, but since I knew Floyd wasn't there I think
we chose not to take the walk. It was hot that day and the mosquitoes
were fierce. I now wish I had gone to the family cemetery to see the old
headstone, which was supposedly moved to Mastic in 1895. The owners
of the Westernville house have a website that tells a contradictory story
about the Floyd headstone. They say a family letter claims the current
headstone was placed over the grave in 1904. They also cite an article
written in a local paper in 1897 that describes a visit to the cemetery to
see the new stone already in place. There seems to be no definitive date
on the move, who was responsible, or how it happened. The 1897 article
also mentions a local resident who thought the stone may have been kept
at a blacksmith shop for years before moving to Long Island.[213]

In so many cases I wish I had thought ahead when visiting these
sites to investigate a little further. While the Floyd house in Westernville is not open to the public, I think we drove by while searching
for the cemetery. I may have been able to arrange a stop to visit the
homeowners, who are really invested in the history of their home and
the Gen. Floyd story. A refreshing aspect of this chapter is that both
signers appear to be buried in the graves I visited, which will drastically
differ in the next chapter.

---

213 "The General William Floyd House," on generalwilliamfloydhouse.org/feature.html,
      accessed on April 21, 2019, www.generalwilliamfloydhouse.org/feature.html.

XXII

September 2001

When I think back on the grave hunt, some days stick out in my mind over others. September 7, 2001, is one of those stand-out dates. Michael and I had an ambitious plan to knock two more off the list by going to Baltimore, Maryland, and Dover, Delaware.

The Baltimore trip was a return visit in search of Samuel Chase's grave. I found the Old St. Paul's Cemetery before, but had encountered a locked gate. The situation here was similar to the search for John Morton in Chester, Pennsylvania, and even Christ Church in Philadelphia, where the church and cemetery are not next to each other. This made it tricky sometimes to find the graveyards, but was customary long ago to have burial grounds separate from the church building. The gate is necessary for preservation purposes.

Locked gates were a constant struggle on this hunt. Thankfully, this particular gate had a key linked to the cemetery caretaker. Connections to historic Baltimore proved to be an in through this gate. Besides Samuel Chase, members of the Armistead family were buried in Old St. Paul's. George Armistead was famous as the commander at Fort McHenry at the 1814 battle when "The Star-Spangled Banner" was written. His nephew Lewis Armistead was mortally wounded during Pickett's Charge on the third day of the Battle of Gettysburg.[214] Having spent years living and working in Gettysburg, I knew people who had done research on Armistead. Wayne Motts, a local historian, wrote a biography about Lewis Armistead, so I asked if he knew a way into the cemetery. He recommended I contact the cemetery caretaker, Rick Tomlinson. I called and arranged a meeting. He was great about showing us around and telling us stories about the cemetery. He also said he had requests from others on a similar quest to find all the signers' graves.

Samuel Chase was an interesting character. My introduction to him, like my introduction to most of these fellows, was the musical 1776. When I first saw it on stage at a local theater when I was in junior high school, I was struck by the fact that the actor portraying Chase was actually eating fried chicken during his scenes. I wonder how much weight actors playing Chase over the years have gained in the name of theater. Chase was described as a heavy-set man, with the nickname of "Old Bacon Face," because when he got mad or excited, his face turned red.[215]

A newspaper described Samuel Chase:

A FACE FULL, FLORID, AND BY THE MULTITUDE, DENOMINATED
HANDSOME—A COUNTENANCE BOLD, ASSUMING AND

---

214 "Old St. Paul's Cemetery," on findagrave.com/cemetery/644048/old-saint-pauls-cemetery, accessed on April 21, 2019, findagrave.com/cemetery/644048/old-saint-pauls-cemetery.

215 "Samuel Chase," on dsdi1776.com/signers-by-state/samuel-chase, accessed on April 21, 2019, dsdi1776.com/signers-by-state/samuel-chase/.

OPPRESSIVE—AN EYE WHICH AFFECTS TO SCRUTINIZE THE INNERMOST RECESSES OF THE SOUL, BUT WHEN MET WITH ASSURANCE, IS CAST DOWN, OR AVERTED—STATURE TOWERING, NEVERTHELESS IMPOSING AWE—THE WHOLE EXTERIOR EXPRESSIVE OF ARDENT PASSION, AND OF A MIND IN WHICH THERE IS MUCH TO DAZZLE, MUCH TO BE DEPLORED, SOMETHING TO BE DESPISED, AND NOT A LITTLE TO BE RESPECTED.[216]

Chase was involved in many aspects of Maryland's political scene. Though he signed the Declaration, he did not participate in the Constitutional Convention, and was opposed to the final product. He feared states would lose their ability to make their own decisions and citizens would lose individual rights. He eventually changed his mind and supported the Federalist Party in hopes of earning a seat on the Supreme Court, which he did in 1796. After Jefferson was elected president in 1800, he wanted to appoint similar-minded men to the court. In 1804, looking to rid the Supreme Court of Federalists, Jefferson asked members of his party to investigate Chase. This led to impeachment proceedings. After a trial, Chase was acquitted and remained on the Supreme Court until his death in 1811.[217]

Chase died in Baltimore at age 70, and as a member of St. Paul's Church where his father had been a rector, he requested burial in the church cemetery. He asked that a simple stone be placed over his grave, with just his name and the dates he lived. According to the website of the Society of the Descendants of the Signers, Chase had the original

---

216 "Samuel Chase," on dsdi1776.com/signers-by-state/samuel-chase, accessed on April 21, 2019, dsdi1776.com/signers-by-state/samuel-chase/.

217 Ferris, *Signers of the Declaration of Independence*, 46.

headstone he desired, but was later reinterred in a common grave with his father and second wife, Kitty. Today's headstone names all three and has a large crack through the stone.[218]

I felt a real sense of accomplishment after the visit to St. Paul's. It always felt great to find a grave that required some extra effort. Since we had to call and make an appointment and someone had to open the gate and show us around, I felt like we really earned this one. We had a great experience there and saw a number of historic gravesites. It was also good to see an organization interested in preserving the local history. After a good morning, we were off to Dover, Delaware.

Fig 86: Samuel Chase's grave, Old St. Paul's Cemetery, Baltimore, Maryland

We were going to Delaware in search of Caesar Rodney, another signer prominently featured in the musical 1776. Rodney supported independence and broke the tie in the Delaware delegation between Thomas McKean in favor and George Read, opposed to independence. It was dramatically portrayed in the musical, as Rodney had cancer and was back in Delaware but came rushing back to break the tie. Rodney was ill, but that was not the reason he was away from Congress. He was working on military issues back

---

218 "Samuel Chase," on dsdi1776.com/signers-by-state/samuel-chase, accessed on April 21, 2019, dsdi1776.com/signers-by-state/samuel-chase/.

home, but did race back to Philadelphia in bad weather in order to vote for independence and break Delaware's deadlock.

Rodney died in 1784 at age 56. I expected this to be an easy find, as his grave was listed as being in the Christ Episcopal Church Yard, not far from the historic green in Dover. Michael and I found it fairly easily and took a number of pictures of the monument over his grave. I did, however, notice a plaque on the wall just outside the cemetery gate, which said that Caesar Rodney's remains had been moved to this churchyard in 1889, over 100 years after his 1784 death. This struck me as a little unusual, but I was just happy to cross another name off the list.

We enjoyed the Dover historic area, right near the State Capitol building. We toured the Old State House and browsed through the local visitor center in search of souvenirs. I am always looking for signer-related memorabilia and found here a scarf with all of the signers' names on it. There is a bookshelf in my house that I call the signers' shrine full of books, but also signer souvenirs like a mouse pad, postcards, frames, T-shirts, puzzles, even a Christmas ornament. As I was checking out with my new scarf, I shared with the cashier what brought us to Dover and how excited I was to photograph Rod-

Fig 87: Caesar Rodney's grave, Christ Episcopal Church Yard, Dover, Delaware

ney's grave. The response I received shocked me. The cashier said to me, "Well, he's probably not really there." My mouth must have dropped, as I said, "What?" She explained that when the remains were moved from the family graveyard on his old plantation property, those doing the moving were not sure they had the right remains. There is speculation that the remains under Rodney's monument in the churchyard are really the remains of a woman! My mouth must have been hanging open at this point. But I had to ask. If not under the monument at the church, where does Caesar Rodney rest? The woman, not realizing I was hanging on her every word, responded with, "Under Runway Seven of the Dover Air Force Base." I couldn't believe what I was hearing. How could a leader of his colony be treated so poorly after his death? How could a grave be plowed over for a runway on a military base? I was shocked!

This was a huge turning point in the grave hunt. The reader has already encountered many bizarre and unbelievable stories about these signers' final resting places. Until this point in the search though, all I was concerned with was finding the grave and taking the picture. Now a whole new world opened up. It wasn't just about taking the photo anymore. I questioned whether a signer really was buried in the spot I had visited, or if that was the original grave location. I paid attention to the date the cemetery opened and the date the signer died, often finding discrepancies. Part of the reason it took me so long to finish this project was after hearing the Rodney story, I wanted to go back and further investigate those I simply snapped a picture of, wondering if there was a deeper story. Often there was more to it, as evidenced by the collection of stories here. It never occurred to me that bodies were moved after burial, or never marked in the first place.

When he died, Rodney was buried on the family property. His will requested that his brother mark his grave and build a brick wall around the family graveyard. Rodney never married. His brother lost his money in supporting the Revolution and was in debtors' prison when Rodney died. To cover expenses, the family property was sold without ever marking the graveyard. Rodney's remains and those of other family members were lost for years.[219]

How then did Rodney end up with a fancy monument in a churchyard claiming his burial site? According to a 2007 Delawareonline.com article titled, "Where is Caesar Rodney Really Buried?":

> MANY YEARS LATER, LEGEND SAYS, SOME UNIDENTIFIED DOVER MEN (SAID TO INCLUDE LAWYERS AND LAWMAKERS) WERE DRINKING AND DISCUSSING CAESAR RODNEY WHEN THEY DEEMED HIS UNMARKED GRAVE UNSUITABLY UNDIGNIFIED. IN PATRIOTIC AND/OR DRUNKEN FERVOR, THEY SUPPOSEDLY TRESPASSED ON THE FORMER RODNEY LAND, DUG 'TIL THEY GOT SOME BONES AND REBURIED THEM BY THE CHURCH THAT NIGHT BY MOONLIGHT.[220]

Just when I thought I had heard all the crazy signers' graves stories I could handle, a new one appeared. While the article said it was based on legend, I have not found another explanation for how Rodney's supposed grave ended up in the Dover churchyard. Most sources agree that the remains under the monument at Christ Church do not belong to Caesar Rodney. If he was never moved, his remains rest where originally buried on the family plantation called Byfield, near the Dover Air Force Base. A state marker was placed in 1997 to identify the site of the property, claiming the family cemetery is about a mile away in a field.[221]

219 Robin Brown, "A Grave Mystery: Where is Caesar Rodney Really Buried?" *The News Journal*, Wilmington, Delaware, April 24, 2007.

220 Robin Brown, "A Grave Mystery: Where is Caesar Rodney Really Buried?" *The News Journal*, Wilmington, Delaware, April 24, 2007, accessed May 17, 2019.

221 J.L. Miller, "213 Years Later, Rodney Remains Elusive," *The News Journal*, Wilmington, DE, May 1, 1997.

According to Russ McCabe, who worked at the Delaware Public Archives, the location of the Rodney family plot was confirmed in 1979 when a tractor broke open a brick tomb. At least 60 people were found buried there, including Caesar Rodney. McCabe worked with others to meet with the property owners and discuss marking the gravesite and allowing for visitation. He indicated the owners feared losing the ability to hunt on the property if public access was allowed. McCabe felt strongly that this area should be marked to honor the lasting contributions of Caesar Rodney to Delaware and the nation. He cited interest from archaeologists in verifying Rodney's remains. Knowing that Rodney had been buried with his sword would hopefully help to identify him. McCabe was quoted in a newspaper article as saying, "Old Caesar Rodney still lies under a field of potatoes."[222]

My friend Bert and I made another trip to Dover a few years ago in search of the Rodney family plot. I found a Boy Scout hike online that gave directions to the Byfield site, Rodney's property. We found the historic marker, but had a frustrating time from there, trying to establish where the property may have been. We were definitely in the vicinity, but never nailed down exactly where Rodney was buried. Hopefully, we can find it another time.

This whole situation seems unbelievable. A leading citizen of his colony who was involved in politics and the military rests in an unmarked grave in the middle of a field. Interested historians today want to remedy this problem and can't find a proper resolution. A beautiful monument in a churchyard leads people to believe Rodney is buried there, but he is not. It is like a comedy of errors, yet should be a simple solution to honor

---

222   J.L. Miller, "213 Years Later, Rodney Remains Elusive," *The News Journal*, Wilmington, DE, May 1, 1997.

a heroic statesman who did so much for the cause, especially the daring trip to Philadelphia to break his colony's tie vote for independence.

This trip made me rethink the previous grave visits and what stories might be behind them. Taking the picture was not enough. There could be so much more to these grave stories that I had not realized. I wanted to go back and investigate more. It would take me a while though, as history took a back seat to current events. We took this trip to Baltimore and Dover the weekend before September 11, 2001.

XXIII

Back to Clymer

I was pretty sure I had found George Clymer's grave on my visit
to Trenton, but was confronted with the locked gate. I put it on
the list of places to return to with reinforcements. Michael graciously agreed to stop in Trenton on one of our Revolutionary
War-themed weekend trips. We found the Quaker Meeting House on
the corner. I pointed out where I thought Clymer's grave was located
under a tree. I showed Michael where I thought he might be able to climb
over the fence. Apparently I had forgotten one aspect of this fence—the
points on top. One of the great quotes from the grave hunt came as
Michael jumped over the pointy fence. He felt this particular act might
"threaten his manhood," something I had not considered in my eagerness
to get a close-up picture of George Clymer's grave.

Once safely over the fence, Michael confirmed the grave under the
tree. As I stood by the fence asking what the stone said on it and telling
him to take photos from multiple angles as I would do, I started getting

a bit sad. I was thankful to be getting the photos, glad that I didn't hurt myself climbing over the fence, and glad that Michael's manhood survived. But this was my grave hunt, and I felt bad that I wasn't taking the photos myself. I started whining from my side of the fence about how I should really be taking my own photos. Michael demonstrated real patience through all of this. Here he was doing me a huge favor and I was complaining. We even took a picture of me looking like I might climb over the fence. My whining was pretty pitiful though, as I was ultimately getting what I wanted—close-up photos and confirmation of Clymer's grave.

After sufficiently documenting the grave at the Trenton Quaker Meeting House, Michael climbed back over the fence, and we headed to the car. We were walking along the fence across the yard from the grave when Michael noticed a gate which miraculously opened and led us right into the yard. All that drama of climbing over the fence and my whining about not taking my own pictures was for nothing. I ran in and snapped up a bunch of my own photos. This was before digital cameras, so I can't imagine how many of the same shot we both took that day. This would remain one of the better grave hunt stories over the years.

Fig 88: Jen pretending to climb the fence, Friends Meeting House,
Trenton, New Jersey (photo by Michael Kelly)

Fig 89 and 90: George Clymer's grave, Friends Meeting House, Trenton, New Jersey

Fig 91: Michael at open gate, Friends
Meeting House, Trenton, New Jersey

I would revisit Trenton with Michael, Bert, and my mom years later as Michael was researching the Revolutionary War. We walked all over town, trying to figure out where troops fought. Since we found ourselves near the Quaker Meeting House, we decided to relive this great moment in the grave hunt and pay a visit.

The fence wasn't quite as we remembered it, but the side gate was still there. We paid our respects to George Clymer. We noticed a car in the parking lot and a woman eventually exited the building. Never a shy group, we struck up a conversation, and she told us she was part of a yoga class there. She had locked up the building, but seeing our interest in the history, she graciously opened it up and let us look inside. The meeting house had great architectural features, and while she wasn't an expert on the building, she indulged us in the chance to look around and take pictures. The website dates the original part of the building to 1739 and claims both the British and the colonists used the building at separate times during the Revolutionary War.[223]

On a table was an information sheet about George Clymer. There was only one copy, so I didn't feel right taking it, but I took a photo of the author's name. I looked him up online, sent an email, and received a copy of the information sheet very quickly. Frederick Millner had

---

223 "Historical Picture," on fgcquaker.org/cloud/trenton-friends-meeting/pages/historical-picture, accessed on April 21, 2019, www.fgcquaker.org/cloud/trenton-friends-meeting/pages/historical-picture.

written the paper about why George Clymer was buried in the Trenton Quaker Friends Meeting House yard when he was not a Quaker or from Trenton.[224]

Clymer died in Morrisville, Pennsylvania, at a home named Summerseat. Michael, Bert, and I visited the outside of the home, preserved today as a local historic site. George Washington had stayed there prior to the Battle of Trenton.[225] Two signers had owned the house, Robert Morris from 1791-1798 and George Clymer from 1798-1805. Clymer had given the house to his son, whom he was visiting when he died in 1813.[226] It is a great old house.

According to the article that Frederick Millner cites in his paper, Clymer died in January when crossing the Delaware River from Pennsylvania to New Jersey could have been a challenge. Millner asked author David Maxey why Clymer was buried in Trenton. Maxey's best guess was that Clymer "deliberately chose the destination in your graveyard because of a residual attachment to the Society of Friends."[227] While Clymer was not raised a Quaker, family members had been, including his mother who was forced out when she married a non-Quaker. When Clymer was orphaned at a young age, he went to live with his Quaker aunt and uncle, who did not raise him as a Quaker. Maybe these family connections stuck with him, especially as he neared the end of his life.

Clymer was active in many aspects of the Pennsylvania colony, from politics, to business, and later a college trustee. He signed the

---

224 Frederick L. Millner, "George Clymer and His Quaker Connection," September 28, 2006.

225 "Historic Summerseat," on historicsummerseat.com, accessed on April 21, 2019, http://historicsummerseat.com/.

226 "Summerseat," on hmdb.org/marker.asp?marker=86009, accessed on May 19, 2019, www.hmdb.org/marker.asp?marker=86009.

227 Frederick L. Millner, "George Clymer and His Quaker Connection," September 28, 2006.

Constitution, as well as the Declaration. He died at age 73.[228] He may not be the most famous of the signers, but I will not forget his name. I will always remember George Clymer at the Trenton Quaker Meeting House, for that first visit when I thought in order to see his grave, I would have to be a "climber" over that fence.

---

228 Ferris, *Signers of the Declaration of Independence*, 51.

XXIV

South Carolina Campaign

The great South Carolina campaign of November 2001 was my second visit to Charleston. The first, during the parental trip of 1999, was before the quest for signers' graves was officially underway. I remember one evening, while vacationing with my parents, when we all chose to go our separate ways—Dad to the pool, Mom to the shops, and me, a walk through the historic district. I stumbled across St. Philip's Episcopal Church and saw the sign announcing the graves of Edward Rutledge, Declaration of Independence signer, and Charles Pinckney, Constitution signer. Having just visited Savannah and seen Button Gwinnett's grave, the thought of such a project may have crossed my mind, but I didn't take it too seriously.

As I looked at that sign at St. Philip's, I was eager to go in and look around. Edward Rutledge stood out to me as a prominent character in the musical 1776. As a representative from the Deep South, and the youngest of the signers, Rutledge spoke out against Jefferson's reference to slavery in the Declaration of Independence. I found a familiar problem here—the locked gate. I could not get in and from my position on the sidewalk I could not see Rutledge's grave among the crowded cemetery. It did not occur to me until much later that my stroll through the city was past normal business hours and perhaps the gates were open earlier in the day. For whatever reason, I never returned to St. Philip's during that trip and a photograph of Edward Rutledge's grave and the other South Carolina signers would have to wait until my next visit.

In wanting to complete this project, I looked over the list of signers whose graves I still needed to visit and saw the whole state of South Carolina missing from the collection. I asked my history traveling companion Michael if he had any interest in a trip to South Carolina. Having last visited Charleston with his parents during a hurricane, he was anxious to spend some time in the historic city. Usually, when we plan trips, we jam pack our schedule with so much to see and do that we come back more tired, needing a vacation after a vacation. We decided to take it easy this trip, driving down to Charleston and having a base of operations at a hotel downtown, convenient to the historic area. Our goals were fairly straightforward—to find the signers' graves, tour Fort Sumter, browse through some bookstores, and soak up the Charleston culture. We had three days to accomplish our tasks.

On our first day out we decided to attack the grave furthest from where we were staying, that of Thomas Heyward, Jr. Thankfully my friend Bert had done the legwork for me on this one, finding a Revolutionary War book about sites in South Carolina that gave specific directions to Heyward's grave.[229] The Heyward family home was known as Old House and was located in Jasper County, South Carolina, not far

---

229 Daniel W. Barefoot, *Touring South Carolina's Revolutionary War Sites* (Winston-Salem, NC: John F. Blair Publisher, 1999), 112-113.

from Beaufort. Heyward, the signer, died in April 1809 at the neighboring White Hall plantation, the last surviving South Carolina signer.[230]

A historic study was done of the Old House Plantation and graveyard in 1996. According to this study, a monument to Heyward the signer was placed in the family cemetery around 1920. One source claimed falling trees over the years damaged the stones, motivating the monument and restoration work at the cemetery. I have a feeling that is what I photographed believing it to be the grave of Thomas Heyward, Jr. The map included in the historic study shows the monument and the tomb side by side. There does not seem to be a question of whether Heyward is buried there though, as he died on the family property and was buried nearby in the family graveyard.[231]

I would take a little liberty when it came to finding Thomas Lynch, Jr.'s grave. Lynch had a sad story, as he ended up in the Continental Congress because his father had suffered a stroke while serving in Philadelphia. Lynch, the son, was elected a representative probably to be there to help his father. He had shown an interest in local politics and joined the army, where he contracted a fever that impacted his health. He and his father

Fig 92: Thomas Heyward, Jr.'s grave, Jasper County, South Carolina

---

230 Ferris, *Signers of the Declaration of Independence*, 76.

231 Michael Trinkley and Debi Hacker, *Preliminary Archaeological and Historical Investigations at Old House Plantation*, Jasper County, South Carolina (Columbia, SC: Chicora Foundation, Inc., 1996), 52.

were the only father and son team to serve at the same time. Lynch, Jr. was there to vote and sign the Declaration in August 1776.[232]

Look at the South Carolina signatures on the Declaration of Independence and find the space between Rutledge and Heyward. That spot was left for Thomas Lynch, Sr., in hopes that he would sign. His health prevented that from happening. Both ill, father and son headed south in late 1776, but the senior Lynch suffered a fatal stroke in Annapolis and was buried there in December. Lynch, Jr. returned to South Carolina. A doctor recommended Lynch go to Europe to improve his health. He and his wife Elizabeth would travel by way of the West Indies in 1779, supposedly crossing through the area known as the Bermuda Triangle. They were never heard from again, lost at sea perhaps during a storm, or possibly early victims of that superstitious area.[233]

Therefore Lynch really has no final resting place. At age 30, when his boat was lost, Lynch was the signer who died at the youngest age. I assumed that Lynch and his wife sailed from Charleston when they left on their trip. Since an actual grave does not exist, I thought the next best thing was to get as close as possible. Whenever I saw a reference to Lynch's grave, it would say he died at sea. An important stop on our Charleston trip was a visit to Fort Sumter, the fort in Charleston Harbor where the first shots of the Civil War were fired. The tour required a boat ride to the fort. This seemed like the ideal opportunity to capture a photo of Thomas Lynch's grave at sea. I took a number of photographs of the water from the boat to Fort Sumter, figuring this was the closest representation I'd find for a grave for Thomas Lynch, Jr.

---

232 "Thomas Lynch Jr.," on dsdi1776.com/signers-by-state/thomas-lynch-jr/, accessed on May 19, 2019, www.dsdi1776.com/signers-by-state/thomas-lynch-jr/.

233 "Thomas Lynch Jr.," on dsdi1776.com/signers-by-state/thomas-lynch-jr/, accessed on May 19, 2019, www.dsdi1776.com/signers-by-state/thomas-lynch-jr/.

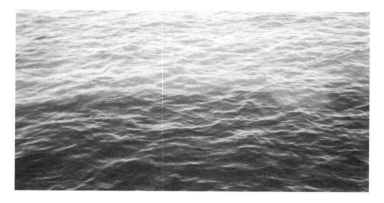

Fig 93: Charleston Harbor on boat to Fort Sumter, since Thomas Lynch, Jr. died at sea

I was always looking for more information about the signers, so I was eager to visit the home where Thomas Lynch, Jr. was born. The plantation called Hopsewee is located in Georgetown, South Carolina. Michael and I visited this home on another trip to South Carolina, after touring Edenton, North Carolina, and finding James Wilson's original burial plot. Hopsewee was built around 1740 and has had only five owners since that time. It is privately owned, but open for tours.[234] We had a lovely visit with the owner, Ms. Raejean Beattie, who showed us all around the home and shared the history with us. She also tipped us off to a neat historic church nearby, off a dirt road, attended by the Lynch family. We spent some time there looking for the graffiti that a young Lynch, Jr, had left behind. These stops were more great historic sites that I might have missed had I not been so interested in the signers. Maybe I shouldn't really count Lynch in the list of graves I visited, but I feel as though I did the best that I could to include him in this collection.

---

234 "Hopsewee Plantation," on hopsewee.com/index.html, accessed on May 25, 2019, hopsewee.com/index.html.

Now we return to the Charleston trip. Michael and I enjoyed the visit to Fort Sumter and spent a bit of time wandering around the historic city. We made our way to St. Philip's Church in search of Edward Rutledge's grave. It was late afternoon, but the cemetery gates were open and the church lights were on. There were a number of other visitors wandering around this old historic cemetery. Many prominent South Carolina politicians are buried in the churchyard, so it was a great place to explore. We must have been so busy looking at all the stones that we didn't notice the church lights go out and the gate we had entered through close. There was at least one other person in there with us, and a number of folks on the outside looking in wondering what would happen to us. During the search, I often complained about the locked gate keeping me out of graveyards, but this time, a locked gate might have kept me in a graveyard.

I'm not normally superstitious, but the idea of staying overnight in an old cemetery did not exactly appeal to me. While I didn't think about it then, I have since seen many references to the St. Philip's churchyard being haunted. I lived in a number of houses in Gettysburg that were supposedly haunted. Michael and I took a walk one year down West Confederate Avenue on the Gettysburg battlefield on Halloween to tempt fate and see if any ghosts appeared. Never have I seen anything to make me believe, but maybe because I don't believe, ghosts don't appear to me. In any case, I was certainly not up for seeing whether this cemetery was haunted. I started to wonder how we would get out.

People on the outside of the gate seemed concerned for us too. I remember them watching us and looking around to see if someone was still there who could open the gate. It was almost like animals at the zoo, being watched from outside of their cages. Thankfully, it did not take us too long to realize there was another gate that had not been locked yet, and we were able to leave the churchyard. There would be no ghost hunting for us that evening. I am relieved even more as I have since found the story of Sue Howard Hardy, a member of St. Philip's Church who died in 1888, six days after giving birth to a stillborn daughter. Almost a century later a local man took a picture of the cemetery and when the photo came back there appeared to be an image of a woman leaning over the baby's grave. This story is told on ghost tours around the city. The church folks probably don't care to hear these tales, as they have a sign posted outside the churchyard that says, "The only ghost at St. Philip's is the holy ghost," encouraging people to worship at the church.[235]

Enough about ghost stories and back to the real reason we almost got trapped at St. Philip's churchyard. We were there in search of Edward Rutledge, who died in January of 1800 at age 50, while still serving as governor of South Carolina. The current church building was finished in 1838, but this had been the location for a previous building lost to fire.[236] A biography of Edward and his brother John notes that "after an elaborate military funeral he [Edward] was buried in the family plot in St. Philip's churchyard."[237] This implies that Edward Rutledge might still rest

Fig 94: Edward Rutledge's grave, St. Philip's churchyard, Charleston, South Carolina

---

235 "The Photograph of Sue Howard Hardy," on Scares and Haunts of Charleston, accessed on May 19, 2019, https://scaresandhauntsofcharleston.wordpress.com/2012/03/13/the-photograph-of-sue-howard-hardy/.

236 "Our History: A Brief History of St. Philip's Church," on stphilipschurchsc.org/our-history, accessed on May 19, 2019, http://stphilipschurchsc.org/our-history.

237 James Haw, *John and Edward Rutledge of South Carolina* (Athens, GA: The University of Georgia Press, 1997), 274.

where he was originally buried. With all of my experiences, I may never feel certain about a signers' final resting place.

Interestingly, this cemetery had an incident that involved moving a grave. In 1850, John C. Calhoun, politician and former vice president, was buried in the Western Yard of St. Philip's Church, the section of the cemetery for those not born in Charleston. During the Civil War he was moved across the street to the East Yard, for fear of Union troops disturbing his grave. Calhoun had been a supporter of slavery in the South. His grave was later returned to the West Yard in 1880. After finding many signers' graves that were moved, it is interesting to see that trend continued to other prominent people.[238]

We had one more stop on the South Carolina trip and then we would have found all the South Carolina signers' graves. On our last day we went to Middleton Place, the family home of Arthur Middleton. Michael and I were joined by our friend Bert for the tour of this plantation home, also known for its gardens. The property was damaged by Union troops near the end of the Civil War and also by an earthquake in 1886.[239] We had a good time walking the grounds and learning about the family and the property's history.

Arthur Middleton died young, at age 44 in 1787. What may have contributed to his poor health was the fact that the three surviving South Carolina signers were captured by the British in 1780 and imprisoned in St. Augustine, Florida, for about a year.[240]

---

238 "Our History: A Brief History of St. Philip's Church," on stphilipschurchsc.org/our-history, accessed on May 19, 2019, http://stphilipschurchsc.org/our-history.

239 Middleton Place Foundation, *Middleton Place* (Charleston, SC: The Middleton Place Foundation), 9.

240 Dumas Malone, *The Story of the Declaration of Independence* (New York: Oxford University Press, 1954), 231.

Upon his death, Middleton's remains were placed in the family vault in the gardens.[241] During our visit we wandered around the grounds and toured the property. While my friend Bert is serious about history and preservation, he can often be counted on to pose for the irreverent photo while visiting. When we found the Middleton family tomb, he posed for a picture as if he were prying the vault open. Little did I know that there is a story about the opening of that tomb. Middleton descendants continued to live at Middleton Place as an active plantation. As the Civil War neared the end, Union troops came through the property in February 1865. They helped themselves to a meal in the dining room and then moved on to destroy the home and property. Slaves were happy to see the arrival of these soldiers and chose their own form of celebration. They went to the family tomb and pulled out remains of Middleton family members.[242] As Judith Lee Hunt wrote:

THE SLAVES' DESECRATION OF THE TOMB IS AN APT METAPHOR FOR THE RISE AND FALL OF THE MIDDLETON PLANTATION COMPLEX. THE VAULTS WERE THE RESTING PLACE FOR THREE GENERATIONS OF MIDDLETONS, INCLUDING MARY WILLIAMS MIDDLETON, WHO BROUGHT THE PLANTATION INTO THE FAMILY IN THE EARLY EIGHTEENTH CENTURY, HER SON ARTHUR MIDDLETON, THE SIGNER OF THE DECLARATION OF INDEPENDENCE AND WILLIAMS' FATHER, GOVERNOR HENRY MIDDLETON. IT WAS THEY WHO HAD PLANTED THE ELEGANT GARDENS AND BUILT AND MAINTAINED THE MIDDLETON PLANTATION EMPIRE. THEY

---

241 Middleton Place Foundation, *Middleton Place* (Charleston, SC: The Middleton Place Foundation), 17.

242 Judith Lee Hunt, *Beyond the Power of Fortune: The Middleton Family, 1784 To 1877* (University of Florida, 2005), 157.

HAD BOUGHT AND EXPLOITED THE ANCESTORS OF THE
SLAVES, WHO, IN DESTROYING THE TOMBS AND EXERCISING
THEIR NEW FREEDOM, TOOK FINAL REVENGE. LEAVING THE
BIG HOUSE TO THE SOLDIERS, FORMER SLAVES MADE THEIR
STRIKE AT A MORE PERSONAL TARGET. THEY ATTACKED
BOTH THEIR PRESENT AND PAST MASTERS WHO BORE THE
RESPONSIBILITY FOR GENERATIONS OF BONDAGE.[243]

Here the legacy of slavery intersects with a man remembered for his
stance on independence. It seems so hard to resolve that these men who
would fight for their own freedom would deny it to others. This is certainly a deeper issue than I expected when I started out taking pictures
of signers' graves. I never realized how many fascinating stories I would
discover on this adventure. Yet here is another Declaration signer who
did not rest in peace.

The South Carolina campaign
was extremely successful in finding
the four signers' graves. As always,
we had a great time visiting historic
sites and seeing new places. We
would also come away with more
questions to answer and more sites
to see. I could never have imagined
all the historic sites I would come
across when I thought about collecting these photographs of graves
years ago. It was so exciting to come

Fig 95: Arthur Middleton's grave,
Middleton Place, South Carolina

home from a long weekend and have four more checked off the list.

---

243 Hunt, *Beyond the Power of Fortune: The Middleton Family, 1784 To 1877*, 157.

XXV

Easton, PA

The checklist of unvisited signers' graves was getting shorter. I was often struck by the fact that some of those closest to where I lived were the most challenging to find or visit. One that did not prove too difficult was George Taylor, buried in Easton, Pennsylvania. I planned to stop in Easton on my trip home to Connecticut for Thanksgiving one year. There are a variety of routes I can take up the Northeast Corridor, but by going through Pennsylvania I could easily stop in Easton, right on the New Jersey border.

George Taylor is not the most famous of the signers, but he has an interesting story, coming to the colonies as an indentured servant from Ireland. He would settle in Pennsylvania working for an ironmaster, and when the master died, Taylor married the widow and continued the business.[244]

---

244 Ferris, *Signers of the Declaration*, 137.

Taylor was among a number of Pennsylvania delegates elected to the Continental Congress after the July vote on independence, but in place before the signing. He added his name to the document on August 2. He was also involved with the raising of troops for the Revolution, but didn't see active combat. He would leave his public positions due to illness and died in 1781,[245] thus not seeing the Revolution's successful conclusion.

My search for Taylor's grave was not too difficult, in comparison to some other graves, but the slight challenge was the different cemeteries in Easton. I remember thinking I was in the right place, on a hill overlooking the town, only to realize that I was in the wrong cemetery. I did spend some time in Easton finding the right place, and eventually was successful in my mission.

Fig 96: George Taylor's grave, Historic Easton Cemetery, Easton, Pennsylvania

It would be years later, after the trip to Easton, as I noticed other signers buried in cemeteries that were created after the signer's death, that I looked again at the George Taylor situation. The Easton Cemetery opened in 1849, a long time after Taylor's 1781 death. On a return trip to Easton with friends Bert and Ernie—it never gets old saying that—we visited the Easton Cemetery. We were fortunate to find a little booklet about the cemetery at the entrance. It noted that Taylor was originally buried at St. John's

---

245 Ferris, *Signers of the Declaration*, 138.

Lutheran Church Cemetery in downtown Easton. Here was another signer moved from his original burial spot. We had some time on this trip, so decided to go look around downtown on Ferry Street, where the church was located. While the current building dates from the 1830s, the congregation began in 1740. Taylor was a member and lived in a house across the street, which still stands, known today as the Parsons-Taylor House. This was his home for the last year of his life.[246]

We wondered if anyone at the church might have some information about the original cemetery, so we stopped in and talked to a woman there. She wasn't too familiar with the history, but knew that what today was the church parking lot was at one time the church cemetery. Those buried in the cemetery had been moved in order to expand the church and create a school building. The church brochure mentions that in 1889 a new Sunday School building was added behind the church, on what had been part of the cemetery, preserving some of the historic gravestones.[247] We were led to believe that today that area is the church parking lot.

The Easton Cemetery Guidebook says that Taylor was reinterred in the Easton Cemetery in 1870. The monument over his grave was built by local citizens and put in the cemetery after Taylor was moved there.[248]

The list of signers who were moved from their original burial spot continues to grow. Ever since the visits to New Haven and Laurel Hill in Philadelphia, I can't help but wonder if these beautiful monuments, like the one in Easton to George Taylor, really mark the final resting place and the remains of these signers.

---

246 The Historic Easton Cemetery, *Welcome to the Historic Easton Cemetery*, p. 7.

247 St. John's Evangelical Lutheran Congregation, Easton, Pennsylvania, July, 2008.

248 The Historic Easton Cemetery, *Welcome to the Historic Easton Cemetery*, 7.

XXVI

Connecticut: Round Two

Only a few more graves to go to find them all, and two left were from my home state of Connecticut. My dad was a willing participant in the grave hunt, so we planned to visit during a Thanksgiving trip home.

I grew up in the rural northwest corner of Connecticut. My friend Ernie has always made fun of me because he says Connecticut is too small a state to use two directional terms to describe the area. It could be northern Connecticut or western Connecticut, but not both. This trip to find signers would require us to visit southeast Connecticut. We were in search of William Williams and Samuel Huntington. While it may not be like crossing Montana, southeast Connecticut is unfamiliar territory to me. I was glad to have my dad's assistance as we journeyed across the state.

We began in Norwich at the grave of Samuel Huntington. I don't recall us having trouble finding this cemetery, which is unusual, since we would return years later and then have difficulty finding it. The Old Norwichtown Cemetery is a wonderful place for history people to wander around, with gravestones going back to the early 1700s. The cemetery brochure says the Burying Ground was established on January 4, 1700. Buried here is Hannah Arnold, mother of Benedict Arnold. While several thousand burials took place over the years, only about 1,300 stones today mark graves.[249]

Dad and I had a great day traipsing through the Old Norwichtown Burying Ground. I don't think either of us knew much about Samuel Huntington. Fellow Congressman Benjamin Rush described Huntington as a "sensible, candid and worthy man."[250] My dad enjoys historical trivia and would appreciate that Huntington is sometimes referred to as the first President of the United States. He was elected to the Continental Congress in 1776, when he signed the Declaration, but was elected its president in 1779. When the Articles of Confederation were adopted in March of 1781, Huntington was still serving as President of the Congress, thereby one could say he was president when the country began.[251] He served a few more months before resigning in July.[252] He went home to Connecticut where he later served as governor until his death in 1796.[253]

---

249 David Oat, *A Walking Tour of Old Norwichtown Burial Ground* (Norwich, CT: Norwich Tourism Office, 1997).

250 Larry R. Gerlach, *Connecticut Congressman: Samuel Huntington, 1731–1796* (Hartford, CT: The American Revolution Bicentennial Commission of Connecticut, 1977), 33.

251 Gerlach, *Connecticut Congressman: Samuel Huntington, 1731–1796*, 5.

252 Gerlach, *Connecticut Congressman: Samuel Huntington, 1731–1796*, 73.

253 Gerlach, *Connecticut Congressman: Samuel Huntington, 1731–1796*, 107.

Fig 97: Samuel Huntington's grave, Old Norwichtown Cemetery, Norwich, Connecticut, 2001

Years after our original visit to Norwich, Dad must have been search-ing the internet and came across a story about Huntington's grave. In 2003, the Norwich Historical Society restored the tomb of Huntington and his wife, Martha. There was deterioration over time and a story that the tomb had been disturbed early in the 20th century. The archaeologist who worked on the project claimed no evidence of any tampering with the grave. After opening the tomb, he examined the couple's remains and even determined possible ailments. The tomb was then restored, with a ceremony upon its completion in November 2003.[254] I guess having recently opened the tomb there is little doubt as to Samuel Huntington's

254 John Barry, "State Archaeologist Recalls Huntington Tomb Rehabilitation." *The Norwich Bulletin*, February 22, 2014. https://www.norwichbulletin.com/article/20140222/News/140229800.

burial place. A bicentennial biography of Huntington describes the
funeral procession to the church and cemetery.[255]

When Dad told me about the restoration and reburial, we thought we
needed to revisit the Huntingtons. We made a return trip on Thanksgiving of 2012. This time, ironically, in the age of GPS and smartphones, we
had a harder time finding the cemetery off a hilly side road. On this visit
we may have entered from a different spot. We walked past the marker
for the French soldiers and Hannah Arnold's grave, along with a number
of very old headstones. We wandered across a little bridge to find the
Huntingtons' grave on a small hill. It looked a lot as I remembered it,
but definitely restored. We had a peaceful walk around the cemetery on
Thanksgiving morning, admiring the work that folks in Norwich have
done to preserve these grounds. Considering some of the cemeteries I
have visited over this hunt, it is nice to see a town remember and care
for its history.

Fig 98: Huntington's grave restored, Old Norwichtown Cemetery, Norwich,
Connecticut, 2012

255 Gerlach, *Connecticut Congressman: Samuel Huntington, 1731-1796*, 105.

On the first trip to southeast Connecticut we also went in search of William Williams, buried in Lebanon. In between cemetery stops we passed by some historic buildings in Lebanon, including William Williams' house, where he lived until his death in 1811; the Governor Jonathan Trumbull house, birthplace to his son John, the artist; and the Revolutionary War Office, meeting place of such Revolutionary War leaders as George Washington, Henry Knox, Comte de Rochambeau, and the Marquis de Lafayette. It was amazing to find so much colonial history in one small town.

Williams' grave is in the Trumbull Cemetery in Lebanon. This proved confusing as we were plotting out the trip because there is a town of Trumbull too, which is not that close to Lebanon. Dad figured out where we were going, and after visiting Norwich and the Lebanon Green, we made our way to the Trumbull Cemetery, another old New England burial ground. As we entered we saw the sign for the cemetery with the dates 1702-1871. Since William Williams was born and died in Lebanon, and the cemetery existed at the time of his death, it seems likely that he was buried there.

Williams was one of the members of the Continental Congress who arrived in July of 1776, after

Fig 99: William Williams' grave, Trumbull Cemetery, Lebanon, Connecticut

the vote for independence was taken.[256] He signed the Declaration in August. He was married to the daughter of Connecticut Gov. Jonathan Trumbull, who is also buried in the Trumbull Cemetery in Lebanon. Williams wrote letters back to Connecticut about how uncomfortable Philadelphia was in the summer of 1776. He also wrote back to Connecticut about the state of the war effort, as he heard about it in the Continental Congress.[257] He served through the adoption of the Articles of Confederation and later returned to Connecticut to be a judge. He lost a son, Solomon, in 1810, from which he never recovered. He died the next year on August 2, 1811[258] at the age of 80, the anniversary of the signing of the Declaration of Independence.

This was another great day on the grave hunt. A chance to explore my home state and its history, plus quality time with my dad. I saw historic sites I had never seen and walked around two historic cemeteries. This put me so close to the end of the search. Now I would be left with the most challenging graves to find.

---

256 Bruce P. Stark, *Connecticut Signer: William Williams* (Chester, CT: Pequot Press, 1975), 55.

257 Stark, *Connecticut Signer: William Williams*, 56.

258 Stark, *Connecticut Signer: William Williams*, 73.

XXVII

Paca

I was getting near the end. With the exception of Lewis Morris in New York, the last three graves I needed to visit were in Maryland and Virginia, not far from where I lived. Yet the challenge was finding where these last three signers were buried and how I was going to get to them.

I had been taking some graduate history courses at a local university. One semester, I took a historic preservation course with, at that point in time, the chief historian of the National Park Service. We had an assignment to go to a historic site and report back on the preservation story of that site. This presented a perfect opportunity for me to accomplish two tasks at once. By visiting the William Paca House in Annapolis, I could do my assignment and also figure out the Paca grave situation. I had not spent much time in Annapolis, so I was really looking forward to this mission. Paca's grave had puzzled me for a while, so I was eager for answers on that front too.

The Paca House is a great story in historic preservation. After Paca sold the house in 1780 it remained a residence for some time, then a boarding house.[259] In 1901 the house became the lobby for a large hotel, built mostly over the gardens. The Carvel Hall Hotel existed until 1965, when it appeared the property would be sold, demolished, and developed.[260] The Historic Annapolis Foundation recognized the historic value of the property and raised funds to restore the site to William Paca's colonial time period. Archaeological evidence was used to replace the spectacular gardens, as well as historic artwork.[261] I remember the story told of Paca's portrait by Charles Willson Peale, which shows a unique structure in the backyard. This helped to identify the feature that was then rebuilt in the garden.

I enjoyed my tour of the house and grounds and learned a lot I didn't know about him, but I was anxious to ask about Paca's grave. I was the only person on the tour, and finally had the opportunity to ask my question.

"Where is William Paca buried?" The response shocked me. "That's a good question. I'm not really sure." I couldn't believe that the docent had never been asked this question before. I understand most people don't have the same morbid fascination as I do on this subject, but there must be some interest in burial places. We frequently get asked at the Lincoln Memorial if Lincoln is buried there. While I'm sure the guide was well versed on the flowers in the garden and the architectural features, I was surprised that someone working at Paca's house had no idea where his final resting place is located.

---

259 Jean B. Russo, *William Paca House and Garden* (Annapolis, MD: Historic Annapolis Foundation, 1990), 6.

260 Russo, *William Paca House and Garden*, 6.

261 Russo, *William Paca House and Garden*, 21.

I left the home frustrated on the grave front, but with a great appreciation for the historic preservation story at the Paca House. I aced my history class project and learned more about the man. What about his burial place though? If the folks at the Paca House didn't know, how was I ever going to find him? I became pretty relentless on the internet and kept checking with my favorite website, findagrave.com. I came across mention of the Wye Plantation in eastern Maryland, but had trouble locating it until an international case happened. Young Elian Gonzalez from Cuba was caught up in a custody battle and brought to the Wye Plantation in 2000.[262] The news talked about where he was staying. I recognized the name from my search for Paca. After selling his home in Annapolis, Paca had moved to the eastern shore of Maryland and lived at Wye Plantation.[263]

After Elian's situation was resolved, I thought about a trip to the area. I called upon some friends to go along. This project ensured me friends for a while, as I promised those who went along on the grave hunt the chance to get into the book. I have mentioned my friend Ernie in earlier chapters. We became friends after working together in Washington, DC. I convinced Ernie and his wife, Minhee, to join me on a ride across the Chesapeake Bay Bridge in search of William Paca.

I really wasn't sure exactly where to go that day. We crossed the Bay Bridge and stopped at a tourist information building. There I found a reference to the Aspen Institute that is located on Wye Island. I thought we could maybe check there and see if they might have more specific information on finding Paca. There was also the possibility that Paca's

262 Todd Richissin, Scott Calvert, Chris Guy, "Cuban Family Finds Quiet at Pastoral Shore Retreat; Apart from Media, Boy Receiving Little Attention at Wye," *The Baltimore Sun*, April 27, 2000, accessed on May 27, 2019, https://www.baltimoresun.com/news/bs-xpm-2000-04-27-0004280268-story.html.

263 Russo, *William Paca House and Garden*, 4.

grave was inaccessible, on private property, or behind a gate. We were really uncertain about what we might find on this excursion.

When we arrived at the Aspen Institute office, Ernie and I went in to inquire about Paca's grave while Minhee stayed in the car. The people inside were very helpful and gave us specific directions to where we needed to go and said there was no problem for us to drive around the property. That was not exactly what we told Minhee when we returned to the car. We led her to believe we were trespassing and could suffer serious consequences if caught. For the sake of the grave hunt, we had to continue. I'm not good at keeping a straight face playing such pranks, but we kept her going for a little while.

We found the grave pretty easily once we knew where to look. It was a beautiful setting, in the center of a plot surrounded by trees. It is an interesting stone too, in the shape of a scroll. After all the effort that went into finding this grave it felt like a real accomplishment. It was wonderful to share the trip with Ernie and Minhee, as we've become great friends, and I'm glad they were a part of the grave hunt.

Years later, when compiling these stories for the book, I stumbled across an email from the Historic Annapolis Foundation. The subject was Paca's grave. The author claims that no one knows where Paca is buried. The grave I visited was on property that came to the Paca family in the next generation. It seems likely that Paca died at his home, Wye Hall, which burned down in 1879 and was buried on the property in an unmarked grave.[264] Paca died in 1799.

There has never been a dull moment on this search. After feeling a sense of accomplishment at finding Paca's grave, it turns out that what I visited probably isn't even his final resting place. Add Paca to the long list

---

264 Jean Russo, email message to Mr. DeVincent, January 5, 2000, accessed on May 27, 2019, https://msa.maryland.gov/megafile/msa/speccol/sc3500/sc3520/000900/000965/html/965paperfile.html.

of signers whose burial location is in question or completely unknown. An archaeology project was done at Wye Hall in the early 2000s, but I did not see anything related to Paca's grave come out of that study. Bert and I would stop at the Paca stone on the way back from Dover, Delaware, in search of Rodney's original burial place. We drove around the area a little, trying to determine where Paca may have been buried. We think we were in the vicinity on Wye Island but came upon private property signs that prevented us from confirming a specific location.

Having found a stone that I thought marked Paca's grave, I had checked him off the list. Now there were only three signers left to go. The end was in sight, but the biggest challenges were still ahead.

Fig 100 and 101: William Paca Monument, Queenstown, Maryland

XXVIII

The Garden Tour

T he most ironic aspect to me during the search for the sign-ers was how the hardest signers' graves to find were the ones physically closest to where I lived. Such was the case with Carter Braxton, signer from Virginia. Not one of the more well-known signers, Braxton was not supportive of independence as late as June 1776, but voted in favor and signed the Declaration in August.[265] In an April 14, 1776 letter to Landon Carter, Braxton wrote,

INDEPENDENCY & TOTAL SEPERATION FROM GREAT BRITAIN ARE THE INTERESTING SUBJECTS OF ALL RANKS OF MEN & OFTEN AGITATE OUR BODY. IT IS IN TRUTH A DELUSIVE BAIT WHICH MEN INCONSIDERATELY CATCH AT WITHOUT KNOWING THE HOOK TO WHICH IT IS AFFIXED.[266]

---

265 Ferris, *Signers of the Declaration of Independence*, 41.

266 Edmund Cody Burnett, *Letters of Members of the Continental Congress, Vol. 1, August 29, 1774 to July 4, 1776* (Washington, DC: Carnegie Institution of Washington, 1921), 420.

When I first looked up Braxton's grave, it was difficult to find any information. My go-to source, findagrave.com, claimed Braxton was in an unmarked grave. The source referenced a family property named Chericoke, which I eventually discovered was in King William County, Virginia.[267] I struggled with this for a long time, wondering how I would not only find this property, but then an unmarked grave. While not too far in distance from my home, this quest seemed a million miles away.

Then, one day, there was hope. I had searched the internet for anything I could find on Braxton or Chericoke with little success. I had looked in books about the signers for any hints to Braxton's whereabouts. After another internet search one evening, I struck gold. Springtime was approaching and in Virginia that means garden tours. Many counties or towns offer an opportunity for visitors to tour historic properties with an emphasis on the grounds and gardens. In some cases these are privately owned homes, not usually open to the public except for these special tours. While searching one night I came across a spring garden tour in King William County that included Chericoke and another Braxton property, Elsing Green. I am not really a fan of garden tours. While I can appreciate a lovely well-kept garden, I did not relish the idea of listening to people talk about varieties of flowers or the best soil. I wanted to see the historic homes and possibly figure out the Carter Braxton story. This seemed like the ideal opportunity to at least get myself to the site. I figured enduring the gardening talk was worth it in the end.

Hopefully I wouldn't have to endure this garden tour alone. I was willing for the cause, but hoped I could entice someone else to go along. All excited about finally having some information to go on, I asked my friend Michael about joining me. I was pretty sure a garden tour would

---

267 "Carter Braxton," on findagrave.com/memorial/2803/carter-braxton, accessed on May 31, 2019, www.findagrave.com/memorial/2803/carter-braxton.

not be an appealing way for him to spend a day off. Yet he had invested a lot in this grave hunt and knew how important this was for me to complete. It did not hurt that I offered to buy the somewhat pricey ticket for the tour, which included a number of historic sites in the area. I am not sure what convinced him, but he agreed to join me on the excursion. We mustered up as much excitement as we could, expecting detailed accounts of annuals and perennials planted around the grounds. Luckily, we were in for a treat.

It turned out the Garden Week tours are not necessarily what the name implies. One can walk around the grounds and enjoy the various plants blooming in springtime. There were lovely vases with bright flowers decorating the homes. To our great surprise, the emphasis of these tours was as much about the historic homes as it was the gardens. People seemed pleased to share their homes with the visiting public during these tours.

We maneuvered our way to Chericoke and found cars parked all over the property. As we walked from the car to the house we saw a small fenced-in area. We went to look around at what appeared to be a family cemetery. There were only a few stones in this well-kept area, separate from the rest of the grounds. Hopefully we would learn more about the plot from someone inside the house. I managed to take an entire roll of film out in the yard, assuming this might be where Braxton was buried in an unmarked grave.

At this point I was pretty excited to be on the property, especially after finding what must be the cemetery. I felt like I was closing in on another grave to check off the list, one that had been so elusive for so long. The added bonus was the chance to explore a historic site. I still expected the tour to be about gardens and flowers but was surprised, as we entered the home, to have folks available to talk about history.

A woman was answering questions in the first room we entered. I explained what brought me there and asked if she knew anything about Carter Braxton's grave. She said the homeowners were descendants of Braxton's and had recently brought folks from Colonial Williamsburg here to do archaeology work in the cemetery. She claimed that they were 90% sure that Braxton was buried in the yard we had visited. I remember thinking at the time that 90% was good enough for me. Now I wish I had taken this a bit more seriously. I should have elicited more detailed information about the archaeology project.

There were many people touring the house and it was not the best environment for an in-depth conversation. After years of wondering about Braxton's unmarked grave, and seeing references to Chericoke, this was a hugely exciting day on the grave hunt. I may still have questions now but that day was such a victory.

While Michael and I were somewhat dreading the garden tour, we were pleasantly surprised by the lack of flower talk and the great historic sites we were able to visit that day. After Chericoke we went to Elsing Green, another Braxton family property. According to a biography, Carter Braxton bought Elsing Green for his bride, Judith, soon after their marriage in 1755. They had two daughters, but Judith died in childbirth late in 1757. Braxton then traveled to England and when he returned after two years, he sold the Elsing Green estate, maybe because of the sad memories.[268] Michael and I enjoyed our visit to this house on the Pamunkey River with its beautiful architecture and grounds—we were on a garden tour, after all. We also visited St. John's Church and the King William Courthouse. It turned out to be a great day for touring Virginia historic sites.

---

268 Alonzo T. Dill, *Carter Braxton: Last Virginia Signer* (Richmond, VA: Virginia Independence Bicentennial Commission, 1976), 8.

As I have found all along this search, there are still questions to resolve. Braxton died in Richmond in 1797. A biography wonders whether he may have been buried in the churchyard of St. John's Church in Richmond, but states that family legend claims he was buried at Chericoke.[269] The word I received from the visit at Chericoke leads me to believe he was buried there at the family graveyard, but with no marker, there is still some mystery around Carter Braxton's final resting place. Yet this garden tour to King William County felt like a major accomplishment in the grave hunt. Even with lingering questions, I was now that much closer to reaching the goal of visiting all the signers' graves, at least to the best of my ability at finding them. Now there were only two left to go.

Fig 102 and 103: Braxton family graveyard on Chericoke grounds, King William County, Virginia

---

269 Dill, *Carter Braxton: Last Virginia Signer*, 59.

XXIX

The Bronx

The most difficult grave to photograph on the search was another one that was not too far in distance, but proved so challenging to reach. Lewis Morris from New York was notable in the musical *1776* as the delegate who kept "abstaining courteously." In the movie he describes the chaotic meetings of the New York legislature as not being able to get anything done. Sources imply that in reality, New York, with its active Loyalist population, might not have been so supportive of the motion on independence. Orders from New York did not reach Philadelphia until after the vote. On July 9, New York joined with the other colonies in favor of independence.[270]

Lewis Morris was born and raised in the Bronx, on family property known as Morrisania, the name that currently exists for the New York neighborhood. This land had been in the family for generations,

---

270 Scudiere, *New York's Signers of the Declaration of Independence*, 1.

but suffered from the consequences of Morris signing the Declaration. The British damaged his estate, and Morris would spend his later years repairing it. He died there in 1798 at age 71.[271]

Morris' grave was easy to find. According to findagrave.com, Morris was buried at St. Ann's Church which sits on land once part of the Morris family property.[272] It seemed like this one would be fairly simple to find. My first attempt was on a weekend trip to New York City with my friend Michael to see some sites. We stayed with my cousins, Debbie and John, who were kind enough to support me through the grave hunt on a few New York City visits. Michael and I plotted out a subway trip to St. Ann's Church and made our way to the Bronx one cold winter day.

When we approached the church, we found my great frustration on the search—the locked gate. We stood out in front of the church looking over the grounds through the fence. There is a stone marker that almost looks like a grave stone, identifying this as the burial site of Declaration signer Lewis Morris. There appeared to be a tomb on the front lawn of the church, but we couldn't get in to explore. As we were standing looking wistfully toward the church and grounds through the fence, a man walked by with his dog. He sensed our interest in the church and told us that he worked there as a caretaker. We told him why we were there and he told us he would open the gate and let us look around the grounds. What luck. When we came upon the locked gate, we thought we were done, but now there was hope.

---

271 Ferris, *Signers of the Declaration of Independence*, 105.

272 "Lewis Morris," on findagrave.com/memorial/2767/lewis-morris, accessed on May 31, 2019, findagrave.com/memorial/2767/lewis-morris.

Fig 104: Lewis Morris' marker on grounds of St. Ann's Church, The Bronx, New York, 2001

George, the caretaker, opened the gate and took us over to the tomb on the lawn, thinking he was helping us solve our quest. However, the tomb on the church lawn is not that of Lewis Morris, but his half-brother, Gouvernor Morris, who served at the Constitutional Convention and signed that historic document. Not only did we get onto the grounds, but George opened the gate to Gouvernor Morris' tomb. We were able to walk down a few steps into the tomb. While it may have been the wrong brother, it was still an amazing opportunity to commune with a founding father and one with which we took full advantage. George also offered us a tour inside the historic church. What was most memorable to me was walking down the aisle in the church and seeing gravestones under our feet. I remember George telling us that one stone belonged to Gouvernor Morris' mother. The church building must have been built up around the existing graves. The current building dates back to around 1841 and was supposedly named St. Ann's after Gouvernor Morris' mother.[273]

While this was a fantastic visit and we enjoyed George's hospitality, we still hadn't seen what we came to find. I asked again about Lewis Morris. He then told us that Lewis was buried in the basement of the church. I was eager to get down there, but hated to push our luck after George had spent so much of his time with us already. I had to ask. He said he didn't have the key to the basement with him. He was out walking the dog when he stumbled upon us outside the gate, so it made sense he didn't have all his keys. While disappointed in not reaching the ultimate goal, we had a great experience at St. Ann's and appreciated the chance to tour the church and tomb of Gouvernor Morris. George suggested we call and speak to Mother Martha, the church's leader, when we were able to come back and she would arrange for us to see Lewis' grave in the basement.

I felt good after that first visit to St. Ann's. With that special experience, I was confident that there would be no trouble gaining access to the basement to see Lewis Morris' grave. I was living in the Washington, DC area, so I wasn't in New York City all that often. With my parents in nearby Connecticut I occasionally found myself up north. If I knew I was heading in that direction and had time to swing by the Bronx, I would try calling St. Ann's to make an appointment to visit. I didn't have much luck. I usually got an answering machine and I don't remember ever getting a call back.

This Bronx neighborhood has a high poverty rate. St. Ann's hosts youth programs to engage area young people.[274] With all the current issues to deal with, perhaps a long dead patriot is not a concern. When I called the

---

273 "History," on St. Ann's Episcopal Church, accessed on May 31, 2019, stannssouthbronx. org/history/.

274 "Community Ministry," on St. Ann's Episcopal Church, accessed on May 31, 2019, stannssouthbronx.org/community-ministry/.

church I always got the message in English and Spanish. Revolutionary War history may not be relevant to the current residents of this neighborhood. I'm sure with serious issues facing the community, an out-of-towner wanting to visit an old grave did not rate high on the list of priorities.

Before one visit back home, after I had made repeated calls to the church, my mom decided to take on the case. This search really became a family project. She kept calling and finally made contact with someone at the church. We made an appointment to visit on a July day in 2002. When we arrived in the Bronx, we were told the maintenance guy who never calls out sick, called out sick that day. What are the chances? That day was particularly frustrating. Making what seemed like a wasted trip to the Bronx, especially with an appointment, and leaving unsuccessful in the mission was a huge disappointment. My parents were good sports and captured our sentiments in a classic photo we took of them staring sadly at the locked cellar doors that kept us from finding Lewis Morris' grave.

Fig 105: My parents outside the cellar at St. Ann's, The Bronx, New York, 2002

Now the frustration level was high. Two trips to the Bronx without success. By this point most of the other graves had been found, visited, and photographed. This one was still out there. Maybe the folks at St. Ann's had no intention of ever letting us see Morris' grave. I was annoyed and frustrated and wondered what to do next.

Michael and I returned north again in 2004. This time he was determined we would not fail in our mission. We again tried to make an appointment in advance. When I spoke to someone at the church, I was welcomed to stop by, with no guarantee that I could get into the basement. As we drove to the Bronx we envisioned scenarios that could play out when we arrived. What if they said no again? This was our third trip and we really wanted success this time. Michael was adamant that we were not taking no for an answer. He made a plan to speak firmly to someone at the church about why we were there and what we wanted to see.

When we arrived we saw a woman working in the garden. Surely a gardener would have a key to the basement. We were feeling optimistic already. We approached the gardener and explained our mission. She said she was a volunteer and she didn't have a key to the basement. She felt confident that if we went inside we could find the church handyman Shelley, who could take us to the basement.

We went inside the church, where Michael spoke with a commanding presence and flashed a business card like we were important people. It worked! The woman went in search of Shelley, who came over to us and led us to the basement. We explained our interest and the attempts that had been made to get here. Shelley seemed a little hesitant about taking us to the basement, letting us know we needed to be careful, as the area was used mostly for storage. Maybe this was the reason it had been such a challenge to get downstairs.

Shelley was correct. I have fond memories of watching my mother climb over ladders in the basement of St. Ann's Church as we made our way to the tomb of Lewis Morris. Shelley may have been concerned about our safety, but finally getting down there was such a feeling of accomplishment. I'm not someone who likes climbing over things, but I was so glad to have made it, to finally be able to check this grave off the list.

After climbing over ladders we turned down a short hallway. Lewis Morris' grave was at the end. Many other family members were also buried here. Yet now, it is essentially a storage area.

It has been a while since our visit to St. Ann's. I can't speak for the current conditions at the church in regards to Lewis Morris' grave. Our visit and attempts to visit revealed that storing equipment took precedence over the historic legacy at this church. While researching history about this church, I was struck by the amazing work done by folks in the community, like Mother Martha, who has spent years devoted to the residents. On our third attempt, I recall a lot of activity surrounding the church. It is obviously a special place in the community for those in need and apparently hosts a variety of programs to help those struggling. I can certainly see why the upkeep of the graves in the basement is not a top priority. I wonder if there isn't a way to inspire those folks attending the church to take some interest in the history that happened around their neighborhood. I've seen some towns take pride in their history and rally around to preserve it, like the Norwich Cemetery in Connecticut or Congressional Cemetery in Washington, DC. I also realize the accessibility issue in getting into the basement. It is not the ideal situation for visitors to climb down the steps. Safety is a concern there. The Morris family played a big role in this community for generations. While they are remembered with the plaque on the lawn and Gouvernor's tomb out front, it is somewhat disappointing that Lewis Morris' grave is hidden away and used for storing supplies.

Beyond the conditions here, I was overjoyed to complete this mission. Multiple trips, unanswered phone calls, and locked gates all contributed to the great feeling of accomplishment when we finally climbed over ladders in the church basement and found Lewis Morris' grave. This put me one step closer to reaching my goal of visiting all the signers' graves.

Fig 106: Lewis Morris' tomb, St. Ann's Church, The Bronx, New York, 2004

Fig 107: Lewis Morris' tomb down the hall, St. Ann's Church, The Bronx, New York, 2004

XXX

The Final Chapter

Over the course of this project, it always struck me as funny that some of the tougher graves to find and photograph were located closest to my current home in Northern Virginia. My biggest problem has been locked gates and private property. While I'm extremely interested in successfully completing my mission, I'm certainly not out to commit any crimes in the process.

Thus, this leaves the last of the graves to find—that of Charles Carroll of Carrollton, in Maryland. Ironically, Carroll was the last of the signers to die, in 1832. I sensed from the beginning that this might be the greatest challenge. On a trip through Maryland with Michael, we stopped at a visitor center. When I mentioned the name of the home where Carroll was buried, Doughoregan Manor, it took quite a while for a local information person to even hazard a guess as to where the property was located. Once I narrowed down the city, outside of Baltimore, I called the local historical society for some help.

In talking to the gentleman there, I was less than optimistic about the prospect ahead of me. He was able to give me the name and address of the home of Charles Carroll, which is currently owned by a descendant of the Carroll family. In the Revolutionary War era, the Carrolls were a very wealthy family, with numerous properties throughout Maryland, and Carroll is often cited as the wealthiest of the Declaration signers. His other claim to fame, along with his long life, is that he was the only signer who was Catholic.[275]

Back to modern times. The Howard County Historical Society employee let me know that Philip Carroll, who lived then at Doughoregan Manor, was not often one to share his property and may not be very helpful in my mission. His suggestion was to write a letter to Carroll explaining my plight and maybe he would be willing to let me visit.

This idea of Carroll not wanting to be bothered was further evidenced by an article in the *Washington Post* that dealt with the Carroll family and its historic properties in Maryland. Carroll and his family members issued no comments for the article.[276] To me, this seemed to further show that one might not be eagerly welcomed to see Charles Carroll's grave and share in the family history.

As I checked more and more signers' graves off the list, friends kept asking me how I could not have been to some that are so close by. The fear of being denied access to this Maryland grave and somehow falling short of my goal put a damper on the project. A co-worker reminded me that even if I couldn't find and photograph all the graves, I should not let that discourage me from compiling the stories and feeling satisfied with

---

275 Ferris, *Signers of the Declaration of Independence*, 43.

276 Susan DeFord, "Where the Past and Future Collide Family Seeks Millions to Help Preserve Historic Md. Estate," *Washington Post*. February 15, 2006, accessed on May 31, 2019, www.washingtonpost.com/archive/local/2006/02/15/where-the-past-and-future-collide-span-classbankheadfamily-seeks-millions-to-help-preserve-historic-md-estatespan/fccac47b-8d46-4832-937b-027be1b341e2/?utm_term=.937d3b225e5d.

what I have accomplished. But subconsciously, and even consciously, I know I put off contacting Carroll for fear of his response.

After finding Carter Braxton, my other great challenge nearby, I knew I could not put off the inevitable any longer. While I was advised to write to Mr. Carroll, my thought was that in writing a letter, I would be asking for a response. If I'm going to bother someone and request a favor, the last thing to do would be to further impose by seeking a written response. Since I feared the worst, that I wouldn't even get an answer, I chose a phone call. It wouldn't require any effort as far as a written reply. Not that I really felt that this would make or break my chance of approval.

A quick call to information provided the phone number. I phoned late one weekday afternoon and was surprised when Mr. Carroll answered. I explained my project and braced myself for his answer. I had hoped by saying I had visited all the other signers' graves, that maybe it would help my cause. But, Carroll explained his position. I recall exactly what he said. "You have no idea how many people are doing similar projects and how many schoolchildren want to do grave rubbings. Since the grave is located in my residence, I must maintain some form of privacy." In one minute, my great fear as far as the project was concerned, had been realized.

The gentleman was cordial, and I imagine, if I were constantly being asked to open my house to strangers, I may feel the same way. But a part of me was extremely disappointed that my quest would fall one short.

I thought of the others who had opened their property and proudly showed off the family history and wished Carroll felt the same way. At the same time though, I respected his position. After I digested the call and realized that this project that had consumed so many years and hundreds of miles up and down the East Coast was as complete as it would get, I felt the need to share this disappointment with others who'd been along for the ride. I called home and told my mother, who seemed ready to storm the Doughoregan Manor. Certainly the man is entitled to his privacy and to preserve his family history as he sees fit. I have no plans to try and sneak on the property. I'm more fascinated than ever in this site, but it is not worth trespassing charges. I have plenty of information to digest with the other sites I visited.

As I finally finished compiling the stories of the signers' search, I looked up Philip Carroll and found that he died in 2010.[277] While the thought has crossed my mind to check with the next generation after all this time, I'm resigned to this being the one grave I have not visited. It seems an appropriate ending that the one unseen is the last of the signers to die. I have learned so much and explored so many historic sites that I would not have seen had I not undertaken this project. With almost half of the signers moved from their original graves or never clearly identified, this surprising element of the story made the search more than just a photo opportunity. It has been such an adventure, with so many questions still to answer about these patriots and their final resting places.

---

277 Larry Carson, "Philip Carroll of Ellicott City Family and Doughoregan Manor, dies," The Baltimore Sun, September 8, 2010, accessed on May 31, 2019, www.baltimoresun.com/maryland/howard/bs-xpm-2010-09-08-bs-ho-carroll-death-20100908-story.html.

BIBLIOGRAPHY

Books:

Bacon, Edwin Monroe. *Bacon's Dictionary of Boston*. Boston, MA: Houghton, Mifflin and Company, 1886.

Bakeless, John and Katherine. *Signers of the Declaration*. Boston, MA: Houghton Mifflin Company, 1969.

Baker, Thomas E. *The Monuments at Guilford Courthouse National Military Park*, 1991.

Barefoot, Daniel W. *Touring North Carolina's Revolutionary War Sites*. Winston-Salem, NC: John F. Blair Publisher, 1998.

Barefoot, Daniel W. *Touring South Carolina's Revolutionary War Sites*. Winston-Salem, NC: John F. Blair Publisher, 1999.

Billias, George Athan. *Elbridge Gerry, Founding Father and Republican Statesman*. New York, NY: McGraw-Hill Book Company, 1976.

Bober, Natalie S. *Thomas Jefferson: Man on a Mountain*. New York, NY: Atheneum, 1998.

Boston, Mass. Cemetery Dept. *Historical Sketch and Matters Appertaining to the Granary Burial Ground*. Boston, MA: Boston Municipal Printing Office, 1902.

Brewster, Charles W. *Rambles about Portsmouth*. Portsmouth, NH: Lewis W. Brewster, 1873.

Bridges, Edwin C., Jackson, Harvey H., Thomas, Kenneth H., Young, James H. *Georgia's Signers and the Declaration of Independence*. Atlanta, GA: Cherokee Publishing Company, 1981.

Brown, Abram English. *John Hancock: His Book*. Boston, MA: Lee and Shepard Publishers, 1898.

Burnett, Edmund Cody. *Letters of Members of the Continental Congress, Vol. 1, August 29, 1774 to July 4, 1776*. Washington, DC: Carnegie Institution of Washington, 1921.

Chadwick, Bruce. *I Am Murdered: George Wythe, Thomas Jefferson, and the Killing That Shocked a New Nation.* Hoboken, NJ: John Wiley and Sons, Inc., 2009.

Conrad, Robert T., editor, *Sanderson's Biography of the Signers of the Declaration of Independence.* Philadelphia, PA: Thomas, Cowperthwait and Co., 1847.

Day, Sherman. *Historical Collections of the State of Pennsylvania.* Philadelphia, PA: George W. Gorton, 1843.

Dill, Alonzo T. *Carter Braxton: Last Virginia Signer.* Richmond, VA: Virginia Independence Bicentennial Commission, 1976.

Dill, Alonzo T. and Cheek, Mary Tyler. *A Visit to Stratford and the Story of the Lees.* Richmond, VA: W.M. Brown and Son Printing Company, 1986.

Dill, Alonzo Thomas. *George Wythe: Teacher of Liberty.* Williamsburg, VA: Virginia Independence Bicentennial Commission, 1979.

Dowdey, Clifford. *The Great Plantation: A Profile of Berkeley Hundred and Plantation Virginia from Jamestown to Appomattox.* Charles City, VA: Berkeley Plantation, 1988.

Drewien, D.J. *Button Gwinnett: A Historiography of the Georgia Signer of the Declaration of Independence.* Pittsburgh, PA: RoseDog Books, 2007.

Evans, Emory G. *Thomas Nelson of Yorktown: Revolutionary Virginian.* Williamsburg, VA: The Colonial Williamsburg Foundation, 1975.

Ferling, John. *John Adams: A Life.* New York: Henry Holt and Company, 1992.

Ferris, Robert G., editor. *Signers of the Declaration: Historic Places Commemorating the Signing of the Declaration of Independence.* Washington, DC: U.S. Department of the Interior, 1975.

Gamble, Thomas. *Savannah Duels and Duellists, 1733-1877.* Review Publishing and Printing Co. Reprint, Savannah, GA: The Oglethorpe Press, 1997.

Gerlach, Larry R. *Connecticut Congressman: Samuel Huntington, 1731-1796.* Hartford, CT: The American Revolution Bicentennial Commission of Connecticut, 1977.

Hageman, John Frelinghuysen. *History of Princeton and Its Institutions, Vol. II.* Philadelphia, PA: J.B. Lippincott & Co., 1879.

Hatfield, Mark O. *Vice Presidents of the United States, 1789-1993.* Washington, DC: U.S. Government Printing Office, 1997.

Haw, James. *John and Edward Rutledge of South Carolina.* Athens, GA: The University of Georgia Press, 1997.

The Historic Easton Cemetery. *Welcome to the Historic Easton Cemetery.* 7.

Hosmer, James Kendall. *Samuel Adams.* Boston, MA: Houghton Mifflin Company, 1885.

Hunt, Judith Lee. *Beyond the Power of Fortune: The Middleton Family, 1784 To 1877.* University of Florida, 2005.

Kean, Robert H. *History of the Graveyard at Monticello.* Charlottesville, VA: The Thomas Jefferson Memorial Foundation, 1972.

Leepson, Marc. *Saving Monticello: The Levy Family's Epic Quest to Rescue the House that Jefferson Built.* New York, NY: The Free Press, 2001.

Lossing, B.J. *Lives of the Signers of the Declaration of Independence.* Aledo, TX: WallBuilder Press, 1998. Reprinted from original, New York: Geo. F. Cooledge & Brother, 1848.

Malone, Dumas. *The Story of the Declaration of Independence.* New York, NY: Oxford University Press, 1954.

McCullough, David. *John Adams.* New York, NY: Simon & Schuster, 2001.

Middleton Place Foundation, *Middleton Place.* Charleston, SC: The Middleton Place Foundation.

Mitchell, Memory F. *North Carolina's Signers: Brief Sketches of the Men Who Signed the Declaration of Independence and the Constitution.* Raleigh, NC: State Department of Archives and History, 1964.

Nagel, Paul C. *The Lees of Virginia: Seven Generations of an American Family.* New York, NY: Oxford University Press, 1990.

Nichols, Frederick D. and Bear, Jr., James A. *Monticello: A Guidebook.* Monticello, VA: Thomas Jefferson Memorial Foundation, 1993.

Oat, David. *A Walking Tour of Old Norwichtown Burial Ground.* Norwich, CT: Norwich Tourism Office, 1997.

Palmer, Henry Robinson, *The Rhode Island Signers of the Declaration of Independence.* Providence, RI: Rhode Island Society of the Sons of the American Revolution, 1913.

Pothier, Jr., Bob and Lavoie, Ellen. *History of Kingston, New Hampshire, 1694-1994.* Kingston, NH: Kingston's 300th Anniversary Committee, 1994. IV-6.

Rommel, John G. *Connecticut's Yankee Patriot: Roger Sherman*. Hartford, CT: The American Revolution Bicentennial Commission of Connecticut, 1979.

Russo, Jean B. *William Paca House and Garden*. Annapolis, MD: Historic Annapolis Foundation, 1990.

Scudiere, Paul J. *New York's Signers of the Declaration of Independence*. Albany, NY: New York State American Revolution Bicentennial Commission, 1975.

St. Amant, Sue Bratt. *St. John's Church: A Pictorial History*. Richmond, VA: St. John's Church Foundation, 1996.

Stark, Bruce P. *Connecticut Signer: William Williams*. Chester, CT: Pequot Press, 1975.

State of New Hampshire, *Addresses at the Dedication of the Monument Erected to the Memory of Matthew Thornton at Merrimack, N.H., September 29, 1892*. Concord, N.H.: The Republican Press Association, 1894.

Trinkley, Michael and Hacker, Debi. *Preliminary Archaeological and Historical Investigations at Old House Plantation, Jasper County, South Carolina*. Columbia, SC: Chicora Foundation, Inc., 1996.

Unger, Harlow Giles. *John Hancock: Merchant King and American Patriot*. Edison, NJ: Castle Books, 2005.

Vermilyea, Peter C. *Hidden History of Litchfield County*. Charleston, SC: The History Press, 2014.

Wearmouth, John M. and Roberta J. *Thomas Stone: Elusive Maryland Signer*. Port Tobacco, MD: Stones Throw Publishing, 1984.

Wells, Charles Chauncey and Wells, Suzanne Austin. *Preachers, Patriots & Plain Folks: Boston's Burying Ground Guide to King's Chapel, Granary and Central Cemeteries*. Oak Park, IL: Chauncey Park Press, 2004.

Wilson, Susan. *Boston Sites and Insights: An Essential Guide to Historic Landmarks In and Around Boston*. Boston, MA: Beacon Press, 2003.

Wolf, Jean K. *Lives of the Silent Stones in the Christ Church Burial Ground: 50 Family Profiles*. Philadelphia, PA: Christ Church Preservation Trust, 2003.

Websites:

"Abraham Clark," on dsdi1776.com/signers-by-state/abraham-clark, accessed on April 20, 2019, www.dsdi1776.com/signers-by-state/abraham-clark/.

"Benjamin Franklin…In His Own Words," on www.loc.gov/exhibits/franklin/franklin-epitaph. html, accessed on February 23, 2019, www.loc.gov/exhibits/franklin/franklin-epitaph.html.

"Berkeley Plantation History" on Berkeleyplantation.com, accessed on February 11, 2017, http:// www.berkeleyplantation.com/history.html.

"Betsy Ross House: The Flag," on historicphiladelphia.org/betsy-ross-house/flag, accessed on February 24, 2019, http://historicphiladelphia.org/betsy-ross-house/flag/.

"Brigadier General Thomas Nelson Jr," on nps.gov/york/learn/historyculture/nelsonjrbio, accessed on March 17, 2019, https://www.nps.gov/york/learn/historyculture/nelsonjrbio.htm.

"Brochure and Map," on Princeton Cemetery of Nassau Presbyterian Church, accessed on February 10, 2019, http://nassauchurch.org/wp-content/uploads/2016/05/PrCemGuide2016Web-Version.pdf.

"Carter Braxton," on findagrave.com/memorial/2803/carter-braxton, accessed on May 31, 2019, www.findagrave.com/memorial/2803/carter-braxton.

"Collections," on nps.gov/adam/learn/historyculture/collections.htm, accessed on January 24, 2019, www.nps.gov/adam/learn/historyculture/collections.htm.

"Common Burying Ground and Island Cemetery," on tclf.org/landscapes/common-burying-ground, accessed on March 24, 2019, tclf.org/landscapes/common-burying-ground.

"Community Ministry," on St. Ann's Episcopal Church, accessed on May 31, 2019, stannssouthbronx.org/community-ministry/.

"Congressional Cemetery Introductory Tour," on congressionalcemetery.org, accessed on January 24, 2019, https://www.congressionalcemetery.org/pdf/Walking-Tours/Intro%20Tour.pdf.

"Elizabeth Arnold Poe," on findagrave.com, accessed on March 4, 2016, http://findagrave.com/cgi-bin/fg.cgi?page=gr&GRid=4074.

"Famous Memorials in Trinity Churchyard," on findagrave.com, accessed on February 19, 2019, https://www.findagrave.com/cemetery/230947/famous-memorials?page=1#sr-8369419.

"Francis Hopkinson, 1737-1791," on archives.upenn.edu/exhibits/penn-people/biography/francis-hopkinson, accessed on February 23, 2019, https://archives.upenn.edu/exhibits/penn-people/biography/francis-hopkinson.

"Francis Lewis Park," on nycgovparks.org, accessed on February 19, 2019, https://www.nycgovparks.org/parks/francis-lewis-park/history.

"Frequently Asked Questions, Thomas Stone National Historic Site," on https://www.nps.gov/thst/faqs.htm, accessed on February 23, 2019, https://www.nps.gov/thst/faqs.htm.

"Genealogy of John Tyler and his Descendants," on sherwoodforest.com/genealogy, accessed on May 31, 2017, http://www.sherwoodforest.org/Genealogy.html

"The General William Floyd House," on generalwilliamfloydhouse.org/feature.html, accessed on April 21, 2019, www.generalwilliamfloydhouse.org/feature.html.

"Granary Burying Ground," on www.boston.gov/cemeteries/granary-burying-ground, accessed on January 24, 2019, https://www.boston.gov/cemeteries/granary-burying-ground.

"The Grove Street Cemetery," on grovestreetcemetery.org, accessed on February 10, 2019, http://www.grovestreetcemetery.org/

"The Guilford Battle Ground Company," on nps.gov/parkhistory/online_books/hh/30/hh30q.htm, accessed on April 7, 2019, www.nps.gov/parkhistory/online_books/hh/30/hh30q.htm.

"Hancock Cemetery Brochure," on www.discoverquincy.com, accessed on January 24, 2019, https://www.discoverquincy.com/sites/default/files/HancockCemeteryBrochure_web.pdf

"Harriton Cemetery," on lowermerionhistory.org/burial/harriton, accessed on March 23, 2019, http://www.lowermerionhistory.org/burial/harriton/.

"Historic Summerseat," on historicsummerseat.com, accessed on April 21, 2019, http://historicsummerseat.com/.

"Historical Picture," on fgcquaker.org/cloud/trenton-friends-meeting/pages/historical-picture, accessed on April 21, 2019, www.fgcquaker.org/cloud/trenton-friends-meeting/pages/historical-picture.

"History and historic sites," on hopewellboro-nj.us/community/history-historic-sites, accessed on March 6, 2019, www.hopewellboro-nj.us/community/history-historic-sites/.

"History of Immanuel," on immanuelonthegreen.org, accessed February 20, 2019, https://www.immanuelonthegreen.org/History/history-of-immanuel.html.

"History," on architectsfoundation.org/octagon-museum/history, accessed on March 2, 2019, https://architectsfoundation.org/octagon-museum/history/.

"History," on St. Ann's Episcopal Church, accessed on May 31, 2019, stannssouthbronx. org/history/.

"History," on thelaurelhillcemetery.org/about/history, accessed on March 23, 2019, https:// thelaurelhillcemetery.org/about/history.

"Hooper Penn Monument," on ncpedia.org/monument/hooper-penn-monument, accessed on April 7, 2019, www.ncpedia.org/monument/hooper-penn-monument.

"Hooper, William," on ncpedia.org/biography/hooper-william, accessed on April 6, 2019, www. ncpedia.org/biography/hooper-william.

"Hopsewee Plantation," on hopsewee.com/index.html, accessed on May 25, 2019, hopsewee. com/index.html.

"John Adams," on Monticello.org, accessed on March 4, https://www.monticello.org/site/jefferson/john-adams.

John Adams autobiography, part 1, "John Adams," through 1776, sheet 28 of 53 [electronic edition]. Adams Family Papers: An Electronic Archive. Massachusetts Historical Society. http:// www.masshist.org/digitaladams/.

"John Adams to Thomas Jefferson, 15 July 1813, with Postscript from Abigail Adams to Thomas Jefferson, [ca. 15 July 1813]," Founders Online, National Archives (http://founders.archives.gov/ documents/Jefferson/03-06-02-0247 [last update: 2015-12-30]). Source: The Papers of Thomas Jefferson, Retirement Series, vol. 6, 11 March to 27 November 1813, ed. J. Jefferson Looney. Princeton: Princeton University Press, 2009.

"John Hart," on revolutionarynj.org/rev-neighbors/john-hart, accessed on March 23, 2019, https://revolutionarynj.org/rev-neighbors/john-hart/.

"John Morton," on dsdi1776.com/signers-by-state/john-morton, accessed on February 28, 2019, www.dsdi1776.com/signers-by-state/john-morton/.

"Letter from John Adams to Abigail Adams, 3 July 1776," on Massachusetts Historical Society, accessed on January 23, 2019, https://www.masshist.org/digitaladams/archive/doc?id=L-17760703jasecond.

"Lewis, Francis," on registers.trinitywallstreet.org, accessed on February 19, 2019, https:// registers.trinitywallstreet.org/files/history/churchyard/history.php?area_id=4&id=440#here.

"Lewis Morris," on findagrave.com/memorial/2767/lewis-morris, accessed on May 31, 2019, findagrave.com/memorial/2767/lewis-morris.

"Mythbuster Friday: Sleep Tight, Don't Let the Bedbugs Bite" on chaddsfordhistorical.wordpress. com, accessed on February 7, 2017, https://chaddsfordhistorical.wordpress.com/2015/07/04/mythbuster-friday-sleep-tight-dont-let-the-bedbugs-bite/.

"Nathanael Greene Monument," on visit-historic-savannah.com, accessed on May 27, 2017, http://www.visit-historic-savannah.com/nathanael-greene-monument.html.

"North Burial Ground Project," on ric.edu/northburialground/history.html, accessed on March 24, 2019, http://www.ric.edu/northburialground/history.html.

"Old Chester, PA: Cemeteries: St. Paul's Burying Ground," on oldchesterpa.com/cemeteries/stpcemetery.htm, accessed on February 28, 2019, http://www.oldchesterpa.com/cemeteries/stpcemetery.htm.

"Our History: A Brief History of St. Philip's Church," on stphilipschurchsc.org/our-history, accessed on May 19, 2019, http://stphilipschurchsc.org/our-history.

"Our History," on First Presbyterian Church of York, accessed on February 19, 2019, http://www.fpcyork.org/about-us/history/.

"Old St. Paul's Cemetery," on findagrave.com/cemetery/644048/old-saint-pauls-cemetery, accessed on April 21, 2019, findagrave.com/cemetery/644048/old-saint-pauls-cemetery.

"Patriot Charles Thomson," on uschs.wordpress.com/2013/07/23/patriot-charles-thomson, accessed on March 23, 2019, https://uschs.wordpress.com/2013/07/23/patriot-charles-thomson/.

"The Photograph of Sue Howard Hardy," on Scares and Haunts of Charleston, accessed on May 19, 2019, https://scaresandhauntsofcharleston.wordpress.com/2012/03/13/the-photograph-of-sue-howard-hardy/.

"Portsmouth's Historic Cemeteries," on cityofportsmouth.com/publicworks/grounds/ports-mouths-historic-cemeteries, accessed on April 6, 2019, www.cityofportsmouth.com/publicworks/grounds/portsmouths-historic-cemeteries.

"Robert Morris," on dsdi1776.com/signers-by-state/robert-morris, accessed on March 16, 2019, https://www.dsdi1776.com/signers-by-state/robert-morris/.

"Robert Treat Paine diary, July 1776," on Massachusetts Historical Society, accessed January 24, 2019, https://www.masshist.org/database/viewer.php?item_id=3364&pid=3.

"Samuel Chase," on dsdi1776.com/signers-by-state/samuel-chase, accessed on April 21, 2019, dsdi1776.com/signers-by-state/samuel-chase/.

"Signers grave recognition," on dsdi1776.com/signers-grave-recognition, accessed on April 6, 2019, www.dsdi1776.com/signers-grave-recognition/.

"Stephen Hopkins," on colonialhall.com/hopkins/Hopkins, accessed on March 24, 2019, http://colonialhall.com/hopkins/hopkins3.php.

"Stephen Hopkins," on dsdi1776.com/signers-by-state/stephen-hopkins, accessed on March 24, 2019, www.dsdi1776.com/signers-by-state/stephen-hopkins/.

"Story of the House" on menokin.org/our-story/story-of-the-house, accessed on March 3, 2019, www.menokin.org/our-story/story-of-the-house/.

"Summerseat," on hmdb.org/marker.asp?marker=86009, accessed on May 19, 2019, www.hmdb.org/marker.asp?marker=86009.

"Thomas Lynch Jr.," on dsdi1776.com/signers-by-state/thomas-lynch-jr/, accessed on May 19, 2019, www.dsdi1776.com/signers-by-state/thomas-lynch-jr/.

"Thomas McKean," on dsdi1776.com/signers-by-state/thomas-mckean, accessed on June 10, 2019, www.dsdi1776.com/signers-by-state/thomas-mckean/.

"Thomas Nelson, Jr." on ColonialHall.com, accessed on March 18, 2019, http://colonialhall.com/nelson/nelson.php.

"United First Parish Church History," on ufpc.org/ufpc-history, accessed on January 24, 2019, ufpc.org/ufpc-history.

"A Walking Tour of Historic Litchfield," on litchfieldhistoricalsociety.org, accessed on February 3, 2019, https://www.litchfieldhistoricalsociety.org/wp-content/uploads/2018/04/Walking-Tour-Brochure_LHS.pdf.

"William Ellery," on dsdi1776.com/signers-by-state/william-ellery, accessed on April 5, 2019, www.dsdi1776.com/signers-by-state/william-ellery/.

"William Floyd," on dsdi1776.com/members-only/william-floyd, accessed on April 21, 2019, dsdi1776.com/members-only/william-floyd.

"William Whipple," on dsdi1776.com/signers-by-state/william-whipple, accessed on April 6, 2019, www.dsdi1776.com/signers-by-state/william-whipple/.

"William Whipple—Portsmouth, N.H.," on waymarking.com/waymarks/WME6K0_William_Whipple_Portsmouth_NH, accessed on April 6, 2019, http://www.waymarking.com/waymarks/WME6K0_William_Whipple_Portsmouth_NH.

"William White," on findagrave.com, accessed on March 16, 2019, https://www.findagrave.com/memorial/7596840/william-white.

Articles:

Barry, John. "State Archaeologist Recalls Huntington Tomb Rehabilitation." *The Norwich Bulletin*, February 22, 2014. https://www.norwichbulletin.com/article/20140222/News/140229800.

"Benjamin Franklin's grave pitted from pennies needs makeover," *The Seattle Times*, November 14, 2016, accessed on February 23, 2019, https://www.seattletimes.com/nation-world/benjamin-franklins-gravestone-develops-crack-from-pennies/.

Brown, Robin. "A Grave Mystery: Where is Caesar Rodney Really Buried?" *The News Journal*, Wilmington, Delaware, April 24, 2007.

Carson, Larry. "Philip Carroll of Ellicott City Family and Doughoregan Manor, dies," *The Baltimore Sun*, September 8, 2010, accessed on May 31, 2019, www.baltimoresun.com/maryland/howard/bs-xpm-2010-09-08-bs-ho-carroll-death-20100908-story.html.

DeFord, Susan. "Where the Past and Future Collide Family Seeks Millions to Help Preserve Historic Md. Estate," *Washington Post*. February 15, 2006, accessed on May 31, 2019, www.washingtonpost.com/archive/local/2006/02/15/where-the-past-and-future-collide-span-class-bankheadfamily-seeks-millions-to-help-preserve-historic-md-estatespan/fccac47b-8d46-4832-937b-027be1b341e2/?utm_term=.937d3b225e5d.

Dixon, Mark, "How Franklin's Grave Became A Monument And Philadelphians Were Persuaded To Like It." *Hidden City Philadelphia*. April 19, 2017. Accessed on March 16, 2019. https://hiddencityphila.org/2017/04/behind-the-publicity-stunt-at-benjamin-franklins-grave/.

Foster, Joseph. "Prince Whipple of Portsmouth: A Colored Veteran of the American Revolution". *The Granite Monthly: A New Hampshire Magazine*. Vol. XL, No.8 (Aug 1908): 287.

"The Graveyard at Princeton," *The Continental Monthly*, January 1862, Vol 1, Issue 1, p 32.

Grotius, James. "Richard Henry Lee's Grave in Cornfield," *Richmond Times-Dispatch*. September 25, 1938.

Hall, Harry O. "Dr. Lyman Hall, One of the Signers of the Declaration of Independence," *The American Monthly Magazine*. Vol XXII, No. 4 (April 1903).

Honeyman, Abraham Van Doren, editor. *The New Jersey Law Journal*, Vol XXIII (Plainfield, NJ: New Jersey Law Journal Publishing Company, 1900), 328.

Jones, Jr., Charles C. "Monument to Gwinnett, Hall, and Walton," *The Magazine of American History with Notes and Queries Vol XVII* (Jan-Jun 1887), 134.

"Left in Its Natural State", Immense Bowlder Marks the Resting Place of Samuel Adams in Old Granary Burying Ground," *Boston Daily Globe*, April 20, 1898.

Maxey, David W. "The Translation of James Wilson," *Journal of Supreme Court History 1990* (1990).

McClure, Jim. "Statesman Philip Livingston buried in York: 'He said his farewells to his family…'" *York Daily Record*, October 12, 2007. Accessed February 20, 2019. https://www.ydr.com/story/news/history/blogs/york-town-square/2007/10/12/post-141/31554821/.

Miller, J.L., "213 Years Later, Rodney Remains Elusive," *The News Journal*, Wilmington, DE, May 1, 1997.

Millner, Frederick L. "George Clymer and His Quaker Connection," September 28, 2006.

"Monument of Elbridge Gerry completed," *Columbian Centinel*, Boston, MA, August 2, 1823, accessed on June 2, 2019, http://www.rarenewspapers.com/view/557560.

The National Intelligencer, Thursday, November 24, 1814, on bytesofhistory.com/Cemeteries, accessed on January 24, 2019, http://bytesofhistory.org/Cemeteries/DC_Congressional/Obits/G/G_PDF/Gerry_Elbridge.pdf.

"No 16 Tomb of Hancock," *Boston Daily Globe*, October 9, 1893, p. 8.

Richards, Charlie. "DAR Honors Grave Site of N.C. Patriot John Penn," *Spartanburg Herald-Journal*, August 9, 1998, B5.

Richissin, Todd, Calvert, Scott, and Guy, Chris. "Cuban Family Finds Quiet at Pastoral Shore Retreat; Apart from Media, Boy Receiving Little Attention at Wye," *The Baltimore Sun*, April 27, 2000, accessed on May 27, 2019.

Russo, Jean. email message to Mr. DeVincent, January 5, 2000, accessed on May 27, 2019, https://msa.maryland.gov/megafile/msa/speccol/sc3500/sc3520/000900/000965/html/965paperfile.html.

Smith, Stephen H. "Declaration signer Philip Livingston monuments in York before the Woolworth's marker." *York Daily Record*. December 7, 2018. Accessed February 20, 2019. https://www.ydr.com/story/news/history/blogs/yorkspast/2018/12/07/livingston-monuments-in-york-before-the-woolworths-marker/38688561/.

St. John's Evangelical Lutheran Congregation, Easton, Pennsylvania, July, 2008.

Vaughan, Dorothy Mansfield. "This Was a Man: A Biography of General William Whipple," read by author on February 26, 1964, accessed on April 6, 2019, https://whipple.org/william/thiswasaman.html.

Williams, Roger M. "Who's Got Button's Bones?" *American Heritage*. February 1966.

ABOUT THE AUTHOR

Jennifer Epstein Rudnick knew she wanted a career in history after being inspired by her fifth-grade teacher. She grew up in northwestern Connecticut and earned a Bachelor of Arts from Gettysburg College. She has worked for the National Park Service at several sites, and for more than 20 years, has been on the National Mall in Washington, DC, hoping to inspire the next generation of historians like her teacher did for her. She lives in Northern Virginia with her husband, Rich, and enjoys reading, traveling, baseball, and spending time with her niece and nephew.

INDEX